The BEAN
HARVEST COOKBOOK

The BEAN
HARVEST COOKBOOK

Ashley Miller

The Taunton Press

Cover photo: Boyd Hagen

Taunton
BOOKS & VIDEOS

for fellow enthusiasts

Text © 1997 by Ashley Miller
Photos by Boyd Hagen © 1997 by The Taunton Press, Inc.
Illustrations © 1997 by The Taunton Press, Inc.
All rights reserved.

First printing: 1997

Printed in the United States of America

The Taunton Press, Inc., 63 South Main Street, PO Box 5506,
Newtown, CT 06470-5506
e-mail: tp@taunton.com

Library of Congress Cataloging-in-Publication Data

Miller, Ashley (Ashley M.)
      The bean harvest cookbook / Ashley Miller.
            p.   cm.
      Includes index.
      ISBN 1-56158-179-8
      1. Cookery (Beans).   2. Beans.   I. Title.
TX803.B66M55   1997   97-6498
641.6'565—dc21   CIP

*With affection
and admiration to the
nourishing and generous spirit
that is Moosewood*

ACKNOWLEDGMENTS

This book could not have been written without the help and support of others.

For aiding in access to books and other printed material, I am greatly indebted to Marty Schlabach of the Reference Department of Mann Library at Cornell University, to Judy Barkee and Linda Beins of the Ulysses Philomathic Library, and to the fine cooking and gardening collections at the Tompkins County Public Library. I am also grateful to Jon Welch of Talking Leaves Bookstore, who was able to stock or obtain books that I wasn't able to get elsewhere. For access to singular written information, my gratitude is great to the Oiseaux Sisters Library of the Odd, the Shabby and the Discarded.

For their generous help, I would like to thank Pat Braus, Eric Broberg, Meredith Broberg, David Cavagnaro, Kevin Dahl of Native Seeds/SEARCH, Antonia Demas, Mark Dimunation, Eve Emschwiller, Martha Hamilton, Susan Harville, Lawrence Kaplan, Bob Kibbe, Jonathan Kline, Steve Lewandowski, Ed Lopez, Flora Marranca, Jeff McCormack of Southern Exposure Seed Exchange, Janet McCue, John and Louise Miller, the Vermont Bean Seed Company, Charlie Nardozzi of *National Gardening* magazine, Jean Nowak, Joan and Edward Ormondroyd, Barbara Page, Valerie Phipps of the Phipps Ranch, Allison Richard, Lisa Romm, Martha Russell, Deborah Schoch, Jay Solomon, Susan Sussman, Barbara Tonne, Raymond Trull, Ron and Maureen Updyke, Stan Walton, Connie Welch, and Rodney Young at the U.S. Department of Agriculture.

I am grateful to Seed Savers Exchange, especially to Diane Whealy, for patiently answering every query pitched its way and for providing me with seeds unavailable elsewhere. Their generosity with their resources can be seen in David Cavagnaro's stunning photographs.

At The Taunton Press, I would like to thank Helen Albert, Cherilyn DeVries, and Marc Vassallo for their encouragement and good humor.

I am indebted to Lorna Sass for her painstaking and thorough work on pressure cookery.

To Christina Stark of Cornell Cooperative Education, who has contributed unstintingly from her bulging files and her own expertise, I am deeply grateful. I am also very grateful to Keith Waldron, also of Cornell Cooperative Education, for his thoughtful and valuable assistance.

My gratitude to Jillian Hull is immense. Her imagination and her prodigious editing and cooking skills enhanced the content of this book, and her creative spirit inspired its writer.

And, finally, my heartfelt and unending thanks to Gene Endres for an immeasurable range of aid and comfort. His literary advice, patient and informed guidance into the realm of cyberspace, encyclopedic knowledge, and cheerful willingness to eat beans night after night have contributed tremendously to this book.

CONTENTS

INTRODUCTION

It was art that brought the surprising and glorious panoply of dried beans into my life. In 1992, for her Master of Fine Arts thesis project, my daughter created an installation for California's Berkeley Art Museum in which an array of dried beans played a part. She had collected a breathtaking assortment. There were large rectangular beans of bright lavender overlaid with heavy black veining. Pristine ivory ovals were set next to those of Tuscan red and glossy olive green. Some had the patterns of a black and white Holstein cow or a red and white appaloosa pony, while others had the brown speckles of quail eggs. As I gazed at these vegetable cabochons, I was reminded of the childhood tale of "Jack and the Beanstalk," and the idea of trading the family cow for a handful of beans began to seem less preposterous.

These beans were not only appealing to the eye and touch, but like all seeds, they contained a promise of the next generation. Before leaving California, I gleaned my daughter's collection. I picked out a handful of beans and transported them 2,500 miles to the East, where I could plant them in the well-worked soil of my vegetable garden in upstate New York and, with good fortune, harvest their

offspring in the fall. And eat them. And save some for planting next season. Thus the promise is transmuted into the cycle of our ancient agricultural foundation of growth and regeneration.

In this section of our planet known as the Americas, beans do indeed stem from an ancient agricultural tradition. Seeds from cultivated forms have been found in caves in Mexico and Peru and, with recent dating methods, have been found to be about 2,000 and 3,000 years old. These are the same beans destined to become an element in the sacred Three Sisters of Life, perhaps the most successful symbiotic agricultural system ever known. The Three Sisters are squash, beans, and corn, and they were grown together for mutual benefit by the indigenous people of South, Central, and North America.

But this visual and horticultural appeal of dried beans is not all that accounts for their importance. They are also a powerhouse of nutrition—the most accessible and highest source of protein found in vegetables. This is a particular attraction for the many Americans who find themselves eating less meat, traditionally the main source of protein in our diets. This shift in diet was reinforced in 1992 with the publication of the U.S. Department of Agriculture's new Food Guide Pyramid, the first major change in nutrition recom-

mendations since the late 1940s. The new guidelines stress the importance of a varied diet with greatly reduced fat and cholesterol. Since dried beans and peas are plant foods, they contain no cholesterol, and the small amount of fat they contain is polyunsaturated. They are also an excellent source of fiber and complex carbohydrates. All of these nutritional boosts lend these humble legumes an unexpected trendiness in a newly health-conscious society.

In the past, a meal using dried beans meant lengthy soaking and cooking. Today's cook, however, can choose from a number of short-cuts. A faithful standby is canned beans. Other options are pressure-cooking the beans or retrieving from the freezer and quickly thawing a supply of previously cooked beans. When time is of the essence, legumes such as split peas, lentils, and black-eyed peas all cook in less than an hour.

To create some sort of order out of the multitudinous clan of dried beans and peas, or pulses, as legumes eaten by humans are known, I have relied on history and botany. The dried beans that we are probably most familiar with—pintos, Great Northerns, kidneys, cannellini—are botanical-

2

ly *Phaseolus vulgaris,* which means common bean. These and the other members of the *Phaseolus* genus—lima, runner, and tepary beans—originated in the so-called New World. With the European invasion and conquest, these beans were carried back to the Old World and grown out, eventually to assume their place as indispensable ingredients in dishes now considered classics. The pulses that I have categorized as Old World were initially domesticated in Africa, China, India, and the Middle East, and they now cover a wide geographical and culinary range.

It is this far-flung historical distribution that has resulted in the important role that pulses have played in cuisines of the world. Their versatility has inspired the cookery of France, China, Italy, Mexico, and India, among others. Their adaptability has spurred impressive culinary innovation. Bean sprouts, soy sauce, tofu, sweetened bean paste filling, fermented black beans, *dals,* chickpea flour breads, baked beans, dips, soups, salads, stews and sauces, and yes, even an ice cream, all showcase this most mutable of vegetables. With today's fast-growing interest in ethnic foods, the nearly global dispersal of pulses ensures their place in a wealth of enticing recipes.

The cook will find this book's recipes organized in the traditional manner of an evolving menu. We begin with Appetizers, Dips & Snacks and segue into Salads, Soups, Side Dishes, and Main Dishes. The recipes have been chosen with the interests of the contemporary cook in mind. Most are low in fat, high in fiber, and if meat is called for, generally only a small amount is used for its flavoring contribution. In most recipes calling for stock, I have left the type of stock up to the cook because I want these recipes to appeal to both vegetarians and nonvegetarians. To keep the dishes as low fat as possible, I use only small amounts of cooking oil in a nonstick frying pan or heavy, well-seasoned cast-iron skillet. Since I gather most of my culinary elements from my vegetable garden, I believe that fresh ingredients, preferably organic, give the best results.

My handful of beans has taken me from fine art to kitchen art. In the spring, I plant the beans and watch them grow with their almost audible vigor. They twine, they blossom, and they issue their long, slender pods. The germinal contents of the pod swell as the pod itself withers. With a basket full of harvested beans I am already imagining these many-hued morsels as my own medium for creating some savory art in the kitchen.

WORLDS OF BEANS

For many historians, the measure of civilization has been its cities. Prehistoric humans took that first step in an urban direction when they began to supplement their hunted-and-gathered food supply with the deliberate cultivation of wild seeds. Peas and lentils, along with grain, were the earliest seeds domesticated by Neolithic planters in the Near East. The agricultural cycle of the planting, nurturing, harvesting, and storing of these crops worked in concert to tie these protofarmers to the land in small agricultural settlements. These in turn became villages. Through millennia, some villages evolved into cities. And the rest, as they say, is history.

In the chronicle of our world, conquering armies dominate many chapters. The Mongol hordes of Genghis Khan thrashing their horses across the plains, the legions of Caesar, Napoleon's army, and World War I doughboys all had something in common besides saddle sores and aching feet— beans. Because of their widespread availability, low cost, and ease of transport and storage, beans have been fodder for the world's foot soldiers for over a thousand years. Even in World War II, someone who waited on tables was a "bean jockey," and a mobile field kitchen was called the "bean gun."

In this country, we can see beans in their roles as economic indicators. In the 1960s, Americans annually consumed approximately 7½ pounds of beans per person. Over the next 20 years, consumption dropped 20% to 30%, reaching a low in 1984 of 5 pounds per person.

The increased earning power of the '70s and '80s was a major factor in this change. As incomes went up, Americans spent more to buy meat, and they got their protein from that, leaving the humble bean—"poor man's meat"—on grocer's shelves. At the same time, the economic picture was changing as more and more women entered the workforce. After a day on the job, a working woman sought quick and easily prepared foods for dinner. With their traditional preparation method of long soak-

Reginald Looked Like This While His Chef Fed Him Caviar, Filet Mignon, Paté de Fois Gras, etc.

But Now That He Gets Plain Baked Beans and Fresh Air He Looks Like This

—*From Life.*

This World War I cartoon is from "The Bean Bag," a trade publication for wholesale buyers and sellers of beans.

ing and cooking, beans were out. But today, as health-conscious Americans seek foods low in fat and high in protein and complex carbohydrates, annual bean consumption is going up. No longer pooh-poohed by the pretentious as food for the proletariat, beans are enjoying a new popularity.

A POWERHOUSE OF LOW-FAT NUTRITION

The worldwide importance of dried legumes stems from several factors, but probably the most important is their nutritional richness. Dried legumes are a powerhouse of nutrition. They offer an attractive combination of high amounts of protein, iron, and fiber, with no cholesterol and only a trace of fat, most of it unsaturated. This is good news for those seeking alternatives to this country's traditional protein sources—meat and dairy products—which are loaded with saturated fat and cholesterol.

Although the terms saturated fat and cholesterol have become everyday words in our health-conscious society, a quick clarification may be useful. A certain amount of fat is necessary in our diets. However, any excess of saturated fat and its sidekick, cholesterol, is harmful. These two substances clog our arteries, leading to coronary heart disease, the number one cause of death in this land of cheeseburgers and French fries. Saturated fat and cholesterol are also major culprits in weight gain.

Let's compare fat in the traditional protein sources with that in beans. In order to obtain 14 grams of protein (about a quarter of the daily requirement) from cheddar cheese, you must eat 2 ounces. This amount of cheddar cheese contains 18 grams of fat (4 teaspoons), 12 of them saturated. Two ounces of broiled lean ground beef will also provide 14 grams of protein, along with 10 grams of fat, 4 of them saturated. One cup of cooked kidney beans, however, contains 16 grams of protein and only 1 gram of mostly unsaturated fat.

Although legumes are exceptionally high in protein, the protein is not a perfect one, lacking one or two essential amino acids. This deficiency is easily overcome by eating dried legumes with rice (or other grains), nuts, seeds, or a small amount of animal protein, such as meat, poultry, fish, dairy products, or eggs. Until recently, the prevailing wisdom was that this complementing of dried legumes with another protein had to take place during the same meal. It's now believed that this is not necessary. In general, if you are getting enough calories and eating a variety of foods, there are enough amino acids retained in the body to combine with legume protein.

Legumes are also a good source of iron. One cup of most cooked beans, peas, or lentils contains about 25% of the USDA's Recommended Daily Allowance (RDA) of iron for women and 40% for men. However, this iron is not in a form easily absorbed by the body. To increase the body's ability to absorb this iron, dried legumes should be eaten with foods rich in vitamin C, such as citrus juice or fruit, tomatoes, dark green vegetables, or sweet peppers.

For those looking for dietary fiber, there are few sources better than dried legumes. One cup of cooked pinto or black beans, for example, contains half the RDA of

fiber. To equal that you could eat 8 slices of whole wheat bread, 4 cups of corn, 5 bananas, or 4½ baked potatoes. Fiber comes in both soluble and insoluble forms and dried legumes have both. Soluble fiber has been shown to lower cholesterol levels and to regulate blood sugar, a benefit especially important to diabetics. Insoluble fiber alleviates constipation and may lower the risk of colon cancer. Legumes also provide significant amounts of calcium (nearly as much as milk) and folic acid, as well as potassium, zinc, magnesium, and copper.

WHAT IS A BEAN?
To answer this question it is necessary to take a couple of quick dips into botanical and culinary nomenclature. Beans are members of the Legume family, an extremely large and diverse group. What makes a plant a legume is its characteristic pod. This pod splits into two halves, with the seeds attached to the margin of one. If you've ever shelled peas, you should have a clear idea of a leguminous pod.

Beans are legumes, peas are legumes, lentils are legumes. And so are about 12,000 other plants, such as lupines, locust trees, fenugreek, and acacia. Although the term "legume," when used in a culinary sense, is understood to mean dried beans, peas, or lentils, the seldom-used term "pulse" is more accurate. Derived from an ancient Latin word for porridge, pulses are the edible seeds of certain pod-bearing plants, such as peas, beans, and lentils.

SNAP, SHELL, AND DRIED BEANS
When I look at a dried bean, I see such a perfect wholeness, such a self-contained universe that it is difficult to imagine its previous existence. Every dried bean starts as a blossom, from the center of which emerges a perfect miniature green bean. This bean then grows into what is commonly called a snap bean. Within the pod of the snap bean the tiny seeds enlarge, becoming plump shell beans. The end result of this process—the mature dried bean, cooked and sea-

The beginning: Tiny bean pods have emerged from the blossom of a Scarlet Runner bean. (Photo by David Cavagnaro.)

soned—is what we happily chow down on in dishes such as Boston baked beans or cassoulet.

Snap beans and dried beans may be the most familiar and available forms of this vegetable, but there is a stage of development between these two known as shell beans. These are the fully formed, but not yet dried, bean seeds,

and they are readily available to gardeners. Horticultural beans, with their red- and white-streaked pods, are often grown for use as shell beans (see the photo on p. 8). They can sometimes be found in farmers' and ethnic markets. Most types of edible legumes are delicious eaten at this stage, but not many people know about them.

Although snap beans and dried beans are merely different stages in one plant's growth, that does not necessarily mean a great snap bean will turn into a great dried bean. Modern snap, or green, beans have been bred for the desirable traits of a lack of "strings" along the seams of the pod, a tender pod, and a long period in this tender

A harvest of shell beans. (Photo by David Cavagnaro.)

stage. The latter trait is achieved by slow seed development, preferably of a small, slim seed to forestall that inevitable bulging that indicates a toughening pod. In a dried bean, however, plump is good and, certainly in northern latitudes, fast is good. This distinction does not mean, however, that you cannot get tasty snap beans when growing beans to dry and store. Many traditional varieties are multipurpose beans, good in the snap, shell, and dried stage.

THE GLOBAL FOOD

On a trip around the world, it would not be difficult to have a regional dish of beans in some form at every stop. For at least 13 centuries, dried legumes have provided inexpensive protein from Tierra del Fuego to the Great Wall of China.

China is famous for the resourcefulness of its people, an inventiveness evolving from a large population having to make do with few resources. An impressive example of this ingenuity is

the amazing number of ways that they have invented to utilize azuki, mung, and soybeans—bean sprouts, bean sauce, cellophane noodles, flour, tofu, salted and fermented black beans, soy sauce, milk, cheese, and sweetened red bean paste. A tally of both the commercial and industrial uses of soybeans adds up to over 100.

Another country that has capitalized on the bean is India, land of *dal*, the Hindi word for split lentils, beans, and peas. Cooked *dals* are an integral part of Indian cuisine, but there is a wide range of dried legume dishes. As Madhur Jaffrey describes it, for breakfast one could have *dosas*, the delectable pancake of rice flour and *urad dal* (split and hulled black gram beans). Lunch might include one of many cooked *dals* with yogurt, cucumber, and some whole wheat griddle bread. At teatime, there might be *dhoklas*, savory cakes of mung beans covered with mustard and sesame seeds. With dinner you could have *poppadums*, crisp and papery spiced wafers, and for dessert, perhaps a fudge made from chickpea flour. Thus, in the course of one day, you can eat five legume dishes without having two that look or taste alike.

Bean consumption in the United States may be rising, but it's got a long way to go before it even gets within shouting distance of Mexico's annual 40 pounds of beans per person. With that country's earliest evidence of beans recently dated to 2,000 years ago, Mexicans have had long practice in using these legumes, which are a staple of their famed cuisine. This cuisine began with the New World natives of corn, beans, turkey, mild and hot peppers, squash, and tomatoes. With the Spanish conquest came beef, pork, chicken, oil, cinnamon, rice, citrus, onions, and garlic. Add a brief French influence from the ill-fated reign of Maximilian and Carlota in the mid-1860s, and you have one of the world's most exciting cuisines. In the culinary richness of its native land, there are countless inspired dishes using the fabulous *frijol*.

From this global hopscotch, we return home to this large country, where the bean favorites are found in regional dishes. New England treasures its Boston baked beans. The image of the overflowing, distinctly shaped ceramic bean pot still conjures up home for many a displaced Yankee. Throughout the South, the bean of choice is the misnamed black-eyed pea. Black-eyed, yes. Pea, no. The city of New Orleans has its own savory specialty, red beans and rice, which is sometimes served in bars at midnight. In Texas, chili cook-offs are an institution. In the West, where the image of a bowl of beans being dished out of a chuck wagon is a common one and where everyone knows what *frijoles* are, an exciting culinary influence has migrated north across the border from Mexico, adding heat and spice and introducing us to the dish known as "refrieds."

And it is from Mexico that the worldwide travels of the common dried bean really took off. Five hundred years ago, the Spanish invaders transported samples of the New World bean back to their native country. From there, it was disseminated throughout Europe and into India, becoming cannellini and *borlotti* in Italy, *haricots* and flageolets in France. India absorbed the red kidney bean as *rajma*. The story of the journeys of this unassuming bean is a romance. From its native growers to the caravels of the conquistadors, thence to oxcarts and camels, and today from 18-wheelers and sea-borne railway containers, these kaleidoscopic morsels continue to nourish and delight the appetites of the world.

THE BEAN IN HISTORY

Planting seeds is such an elemental act that using the word "revolutionary" to describe it could be viewed as extreme. And yet in the sense of the word pertaining to a radical change, it is entirely accurate, for the act of planting seeds, as well as domesticating animals, separates the Neolithic era from that of the earlier Paleolithic era. By taking these first agricultural steps, hunter-gatherers evolved into farmers. The deliberate production of food required a more settled existence, which resulted in permanent villages. This, in turn, gradually led to specialized occupations, metallurgy, writing, and the growth of cities. For these reasons, the Neolithic era is considered the gestation period of modern civilization.

How did these early farmers make the connection between seed and plant? For us, this process is wrapped in a veil of temporal mystery and can only be conjecture. Returning in another season to a previously used camp, hunter-gatherers may have noticed new plants colonizing their old clearing. This previously cleared area could have suggested a seed bed for desirable plants. They may have discovered their previous year's refuse heaps sprouting luxuriant growth like the compost heaps that they were. From thousands of years of experience gathering wild vegetables and fruit, women would have observed much about the growth cycle of these foods. They would have seen that if they were too efficient in gathering, the next year's crop in the same space would be reduced. They must have

noticed that it was possible to exert an active influence on a wild plant's growth by removing competing vines, for example, or by applying water in times of drought. The knowledge of plant cultivation was there, waiting for the combination of conditions that culminated in the revolutionary act of planting seeds.

With the planting and harvesting of seeds came the first efforts at seed selection. As bean seeds, for example, were grown out, the observant planter might have noticed that the most vigorous and productive plants came from the largest seeds. In addition, wild bean pods split open and eject their seeds across some distance, ensuring themselves uncrowded germination conditions and increased territory. This dehiscence, as the

This array of lima beans shows the variety that thousands of years of crosses and mutations, as well as selection and preservation, can bring. (Photo by David Cavagnaro.)

splitting is called, is detrimental to efficient gathering because the seeds are scattered, so seed would be saved from abnormal pods that never opened. In years with the security of a good harvest, beans could have been traded, given as gifts, or used as a required tribute from a lesser to a more powerful group. Stored food and seeds may have been raided. In these ways, year by year, beans were dispersed.

As the beans' range increased and varied, more seed selection took place. With each new location, the environment differed. There were changes in soil, temper-ature, length of growing season, moisture conditions, and day length. With each season, the seeds that responded most favorably to their environment would be put aside by the farmers for the next planting. Crosses and mutations multiplied the range of colors, patterns, and shapes.

In the agricultural history of our world, there is evidence of the emergence of seven independent centers of early food production. Four centers of prehistoric agriculture were in the Old World, made up of Europe, Africa, and Asia. These centers were located in the Fertile Crescent of the Mideast (the well-watered area between the Nile, the Tigris, and the Euphrates rivers), in the Yangtze River corridor in southern China, in the Yellow River region of northern China, and in sub-Saharan Africa. The remaining three centers were in what is generally termed the New World, as it was new to Europeans. They were located in central Mexico, the south central Andes, and the eastern United States.

BEANS FROM THE OLD WORLD

The pulses known to the ancient Egyptians and the Israelites, to the Greeks, and to the subjects of the Roman

Empire were first domesticated in the Fertile Crescent. These early pulses were chickpeas, fava beans, peas, and lentils. Soybeans originated in northern China, azukis probably in Japan, and mung beans in India. The origin of Southern, or black-eyed, cow, or field, peas (take your choice) was in the area of Ethiopia. Pigeon peas' origin is still a matter of conjecture. Depending on the interpretation of evidence, it could be either India or northern Africa.

In a remarkable example of the status of legumes in the ancient world, four of Rome's leading families bore the names of the major legumes of that area—Cicero from *cicer,* the chickpea; Lentullus from lentils; Fabius from *faba,* the fava bean; and Piso from peas. The reasons for these names are undefined, perhaps harking back to a clan system with strong ties to agriculture. What is certain is that no other food category has been so honored.

Beans and ghosts

Because of their roles as sustenance to ancient cultures, beans play a prominent part in the rituals and folklore of the Old World. The culture of classical Greece and

Rome, knowledgeable and sophisticated in many respects, was enveloped in an atmosphere of spirits and superstition. One of these superstitions associated beans with ancestral ghosts and the souls of the departed. Pliny the Elder, the great Roman writer and compiler of natural history (37 volumes worth), recorded nearly 2,000 years ago the belief that the souls of the deceased reside in beans. This belief may help illuminate an ancient Greek and Roman charm for the banishment of ghosts—spitting beans at them—which can perhaps be explained by the homeopathic doctrine of like fighting like.

The Roman year was filled with many officially sanctioned rituals. One of these was *Lemuria,* an annual rite of placating ghosts. During this three-day period, each householder walked barefoot through all the rooms of the house at midnight, throwing small, dark fava beans behind him and repeating nine times: "These I give and with these I redeem my family." This rite is remarkably similar to one practiced in Japan at the beginning of a new year to drive out demons. The head of the

household donned his finest clothes and at midnight went through all the rooms, scattering roasted beans and chanting, "Out—demons! In—luck!"

...and Greek philosophers

Pythagoras, the famed philosopher, astronomer, and mathematician, established a school for his followers in sixth century B.C. An important tenet of Pythagorean philosophy was the transmigration of souls, the belief that the soul was immortal and destined to a cycle of reincarnation until it could liberate itself through the purity of its life. Among the food prohibitions that the Pythagorean mystics were bound by was one against eating beans. The rationale given was a verse attributed to Orpheus indicating that to eat beans was to eat the heads of one's parents. Given the long-standing Greek and Roman connection between beans and ancestral ghosts and the Pythagorean belief in the transmigration of souls, this mysterious bean taboo becomes more understandable.

Followers of Plato also abstained from beans but, being rationalists, gave a different reason: flatulence. To

Robert Graves, writing on the prehistoric and the mythological in *The White Goddess,* it was one and the same: "Life was breath, and to break wind after eating beans was a proof that one had eaten a living soul—in Greek and Latin the same words, *anima* and *pneuma,* stand equally for gust of wind, breath, and soul or spirit."

Pulses and early vegetarianism

Throughout history, pulses have been a staple of vegetarian diets, whether or not these diets were deliberate and long range or unplanned and short term. Pulses are readily available, filling, and high in protein.

An early written reference to the benefits of a pulse-based vegetarian diet comes from the Old Testament Book of Daniel. During an invasion of Jerusalem by the ruler of Babylon, Nebuchadnezzar, Daniel and a group of children were kidnapped and taken to Nebuchadnezzar's court. There, Daniel wishes not to defile himself with the rich meat and wine ordered by the king for their meals. He works out an arrangement with a sympathetic guardian that for 10 days he and three other children

would be fed with pulses and water, and at the end of this period their health would be compared with that of other children who remained on the luxurious diet of the royal household. In a result that vegetarian parents today can take to heart, at the end of the 10 days, "their countenances appeared fairer and fatter in flesh than all the children which did eat the portion of the king's meat."

Buddhism and Jainism, two influential religions that emerged from India, are characterized by a belief in karma. Karma can be thought of as the total effect of a person's actions and conduct during the successive phases of his or her existence. In other words, the way that one leads one's life will determine one's destiny. If life has been lived in a pure manner, after death the soul advances to reincarnation at a higher level. If not, the reverse. Because animals may be inhabited by what may formerly have been and may again become a human soul, a vegetarian diet is required in Jainism and encouraged in Buddhism. As these religions and their vegetarian practices were spread throughout Asia, so, too, were beans. From India, a

multiplicity of *dals* traveled eastward, and from China, the soybean was disseminated throughout Asia with the teachings of Buddha.

The practices of another of the world's influential religions, Catholicism, also contributed to the important role of beans in the Old World. By the time the Benedictine monastic rules were introduced in the sixth century, there were 200 fast days a year in Europe. On a fast day, only one meal was allowed and that had to be meatless. Until the tenth century, when fish was allowed, and the sixteenth century, when eggs and dairy products were permitted, meatless meant vegetables. And the most easily stored and obtainable year-round vegetables were beans.

Beans as tokens

Probably for as long as they have been used for food, beans have been used as tokens in games, gambling, and voting. In first-century Greece, for example, the philosopher Plutarch advised his followers to abstain from beans. This admonition had nothing to do with the transmigration of souls or flatulence. He was advising them to stay out of politics. At that time, beans were employed as voting tokens in the election of magistrates.

Starting December 17 and lasting for a week, the Romans celebrated the festival of Saturnalia, a name that we now associate with prolonged and unrestrained partying. For the week of Saturnalia, boundaries were broken and chaos ruled. All work was suspended, slaves were given temporary freedom to say and to do what they liked without recrimination, and certain moral restrictions were eased. Reigning over this excess was the Master of Revels, whose subjects had to do his bidding. This partymeister attained his reign by the luck of the draw. The Master of Revels was the one who, blindfolded, picked the white bean out of a container of dark ones. In this instance, the use of beans as tokens harks back to the prehistoric origins of Saturnalia as an agricultural rite taking place around the winter solstice.

Christianity muted and transformed this custom into Twelfth Night, when a cake with a bean baked into it is served. The person with the slice of cake containing the bean becomes The Bean King, or Master of Revels.

There are many accounts of beans being used as game tokens and in gambling games throughout the world. In the Chinese game of Fan Tan, a dealer counts off a large handful of beans (or other small objects) in fours, and the players bet on what number from one to four will be left at the end of the count. When the game is over, the dealer rakes in the losers' money.

Beans in folk tales
Folk tales differ from other children's stories because their language is symbolic. In "Jack and the Beanstalk," for example, beans are a magical force that vindicates Jack and furnishes a passage into another world.

In this story, Jack, acting on behalf of his poverty-stricken, widowed mother, sets out to sell their cow. He soon meets a man interested in buying the cow, who offers Jack some magic beans for her. Captivated, Jack agrees to the trade and carries them home. His cash-strapped mother is so disgusted that she throws them out the window. The next morning one has germinated and grown into a magnificent beanstalk reaching into the clouds. Climbing to the top three times, Jack steals in turn a hen that lays golden eggs, money bags, and a magic harp from the evil giant whose domain it is. On the third attempt, he is pursued by the giant. The nimble lad quickly descends and chops down the beanstalk with an ax. The giant falls to his death and Jack keeps the three treasures, ensuring a life of prosperity and ease for him and his mother.

Two additional stories in which a bean or beans play a large role fall into the category of explanatory tales. In the Brothers Grimm's "The Straw, the Coal and the Bean," a bean laughs so hard and for so long at his companions' misfortune that he splits his side. A sympathetic tailor sews him up with black thread and that is why "all beans have a black seam to this day." (As a child, this image never rang true. No bean I'd ever seen had a black seam. Re-reading this story as an adult, I understood that the bean described was a fava.)

From Ghana comes the amusing tale of "The Hat-Shaking Dance." It seems that Anansi, a spider, was determined to be the most conspicuous mourner at his mother-in-law's funeral. This required that he fast longer than any of the other mourners. On the fourth day, however, he happened to be alone where a pot of beans was cooking over the fire. Too tempting for a hungry mourner to resist, Anansi was dipping into them with a large spoon when friends came into the kitchen. Startled, but thinking quickly, he spooned the hot beans into his hat and placed it on his head. Jumping and wriggling with the pain of the hot beans under his hat, Anansi blurted out that today, in his own village, the hat-shaking festival was going on, and he was shaking his hat in its honor and to demonstrate the famous hat-shaking dance for their benefit. Of course, the hot beans burned all the hair off his head, and from that day to this, spiders have been bald.

BEANS FROM THE NEW WORLD

Beans familiar to us that originated in the Americas are an easily defined group all belonging to the same genus, *Phaseolus*. Of this group, four are cultivated in significant numbers.

Common beans

Most familiar and widely distributed is *Phaseolus vulgaris*, or common bean. We know a few of these as kidney, pinto, Great Northern, black turtle, navy, and cannellini beans. The Seed Savers Exchange, a storehouse and network of seed savers, lists over 1,500 common beans. They were grown by natives from the far tip of Chile and Argentina to the present site of Montreal.

From the Americas, common beans traveled eastward to Europe beginning in 1493 with the second voyage of Columbus. In time, they reached Africa, India, and Asia. Their reception in Asia was not enthusiastic because faster-cooking native beans such as mung and azuki were an established staple of regional food cultures and had long been grown in great variety.

Their reception in Europe, however, was another story. Until the arrival of the common bean, the bean of Europe was the fava. Although well adapted to cool European growing conditions, the fava has two disadvantages: its leathery skin and favism, an anemia triggered by an allergic reaction in genetically susceptible individuals of Mediterranean descent. Common beans lacked these disadvantages and gradually began to displace favas. As Old World farmers grew these beans, they built upon the foundation provided for them by their New World counterparts and continued with their own seed selection and breeding efforts. With time, they produced dozens of new varieties of the common bean. Some, such as 'Swedish Brown' or 'Madeira', have completed the circle, returning to this continent in the luggage of European settlers.

Lima beans

The second New World bean is the lima, or *Phaseolus lunatus*, named by Linnaeus for its more or less half-moon shape.

Well-preserved remains of limas have been found in the northern coastal desert area of Peru and radiocarbon-dated to 5,000 years ago. (Work currently being done with the newer and more accurate accelerated mass spectrometry may alter this date significantly.) The large amounts found in Peru suggest that limas must have been a significant part of the native diet.

That they also had great social significance is implied by their representation on ceramics from the Peruvian Moché culture of A.D. 100 to A.D. 800. One image depicts running messengers, each with a small bag decorated with pictures of lima beans. A second image is stick-limbed lima bean warriors rushing to the attack. In addition, there are depictions of these beans on textiles from Paracas, an earlier Peruvian coastal site.

Runner beans

The third bean native to the New World is the runner bean, *Phaseolus coccineus*. *Coccineus* is derived from the same Greek root word as cochineal, the scarlet dye, which reflects the brilliant red flowers of the bean's most noticeable varieties.

Although grown more as an ornamental in this country, runner beans are enjoyed as a vegetable in England, where at least 10 varieties are available. With England's cool growing conditions, this bean's ability to germinate and grow under cooler conditions than the common bean undoubtedly accounts for its popularity.

Tepary beans

One characteristic of beans in the Americas has been their identification with specific geographic and cultural areas. For example, walk into any grocery store in New England and you will find the handsome maroon and white 'Jacob's Cattle', a good baking bean adapted to a short growing season. In the central market of San Jose, Costa Rica, growers offer two local favorites, a large yellow ochre and a small pink bean. In Oaxaca, Mexico, a particular black bean is the *frijol local*. The fourth variety of New World bean, the tepary (*Phaseolus acutifolius*), also exemplifies this cultural and regional identification. It is a bean of the desert areas of the Southwest and Mexico, a bush bean grown out and preserved by native peoples for generations.

One of those native peoples is the Papago tribe of the Arizona-Sonoran borderlands, whose name is a corruption of a nickname given them long ago by their Pima neighbors meaning "Tepary Bean Eaters." And the nickname seems to fit because even as late as 1944 the average amount consumed daily by an individual of this tribe was nearly two-thirds of a pound. In 1919, an Indian agent reported that the Papago, in an arid land and in an even drier than usual year, had raised an astounding 1,800,000 pounds of beans. That they accomplished this speaks not only of their farming skill, but also of the remarkable properties of tepary beans.

The Three Sisters

Taking their cue from the natural world around them, early planters would have noted a diversity of vegetation growing together. Close observation would reveal a complexity of botanical relationships—a vine that clambers up and over other plants but that furnishes shade from intense sun for those plants supporting it, or small plants thriving in the cool microclimate found under the leaves of a larger plant. Native planters adopted and experimented with this multiplicity, eventually creating one of the most successful forms of sustainable agriculture in the world. This is known as the Three Sisters—corn, beans, and squash.

This growing method consists of the cultivation of these three crops in the same field at the same time. The selection of these three embodies a complex interdependency related to their growth patterns, use of sunlight and soil nutrients, harvest, and nutrition. The food harvested from this combination has historically been the Native American dietary staple, food that could be eaten fresh or dried for future use in difficult times, such as periods of extreme cold, drought, wars, and migrations. As well as these agricultural and nutritional aspects, however, the Three Sisters represents a cultural complex. It is the source of myths and cautionary tales, thanksgiving, and festivals.

When grown together, the three plants complement each other in a beneficial relationship that does indeed suggest the ideal precepts of the familial. The roots of each plant occupy a different zone of soil—corn is shallow-rooted, beans have roots of intermediate length, about

The Scarlet Runner bean originated in Mexico, where it can still be found growing wild in cool, shaded areas. (Photo by David Cavagnaro.)

36 in., and squash or pumpkins reach deeper yet. Beans fix nitrogen from the air and make it available to the roots of the corn and squash, which lack this ability. Shade from these two plants suppresses weed growth and retards evaporation from the surface of the soil, and the leaves of all three work together to reduce the impact of rain, thereby reducing erosion.

The Three Sisters also exhibits complementary vegetative growth. Corn varieties, depending on nutrients and moisture, grow from 5 ft.

The Three Sisters complex, an intercropping of corn, squash, and beans, is one of the most successful agricultural methods ever developed. (Photo by David Cavagnaro.)

protein, also lack one or two amino acids. Eating beans with a grain, such as corn, provides the missing amino acid balance and forms a complete protein.

Planting the Three Sisters was an important part of life, and it was done precisely. For example, in *Buffalo Bird Woman's Garden*, a woman born into the Hidatsa tribe around 1839 in what is now North Dakota describes in detail the agricultural work of her time and place. Individuals claimed land to be cultivated and marked it by family groups. The land was then cleared. Hills for the corn were formed in rows, both the rows and the hills being about 4 ft. apart. If hills were closer, when the corn grew and touched the corn plants in adjacent hills, they were called "smell each other," and it was known that the ears they bore would be small and thin. Because of remaining stumps, the rows of the first year's planting were quite irregular.

The corn was always planted first, beginning when the women observed that the wild gooseberry was nearly in full leaf. Plots approximately

to 15 ft. Twining beans will climb 10 ft. to 15 ft. on cornstalk supports, and sprawling, large-leaved squash will shade the ground and suppress weeds, while setting fruit at the edge of the patch.

Nutritionally, corn provides an excellent source of carbohydrates, protein, and polyunsaturated oil. Its protein, however, lacks balance in amino acids. With lysine and tryptophan from beans, this protein is balanced and complete. Beans, high in nine rows long by four rows wide would be separated from their neighbors by a row of squash. Beans were sown last in rows between the corn rows (see the illustration on p. 20). All hills were more or less permanent, used year after year until the field was left fallow and a new one planted.

Tribes in other regions had slightly different patterns. Some varied the number of seeds, while others planted their hills with corn in the middle surrounded by a ring of beans and squash.

Buffalo Bird Woman voices the spiritual element of these gardens when she states that it was "our Indian rule to keep our fields very sacred." The Three Sisters themselves were spirit beings. In a Thanksgiving address, which began and ended most major seasonal ceremonies, they were referred to and thanked by the Senaca as "the Sisters, our sustenance." The Senecas also had a sacred society, the Tonwisas, or the Sisters of Diohe'ko (the Three Sisters), made up entirely of women who conducted ceremonies before and after planting. Seasonal festivals were held as the

Three Sisters ripened. Here, this complex could be interpreted as "medicine," a preventive and restorative force requiring communal rituals to maintain its power. Members of the community reinforced the group as a whole by participating in these celebratory rites.

Do the Three Sisters have relevance in today's large-scale monocultural farming methods? Experiments in Kenya and Uganda point to several benefits of this intercropping. In trials in both countries, intercropped fields of corn and beans outperformed monocultures in total yield and total protein. One study showed that greater gains resulted from high plant populations, while the other indicated that intercropped fields have advantages for passive pest control.

In his thoughtful essay on the Three Sisters in Seneca life, Steve Lewandowski concludes: "The Three Sisters is where agriculture and horticulture and human culture meet. Is it gardening on a large scale or agriculture with a human face? In any case, it is a cultural complex, with distinct but inter-related factors, in which the functions

of planting, harvesting, and eating are more than simple biological necessities; they are elements of a well-recognized sacrament."

Myth and ritual
Because beans were usually grown in association with corn and squash, and because this association of the Three Sisters had an attached sacredness, native myths and rituals incorporating beans usually involve the other two sisters. Often just corn and beans are featured, such as in the Cherokee legend of their origin.

This story begins with the magical creation of a baby boy who is found by Selu Tvya (whose name, translated, means Corn Bean) and raised as her grandson. Wanting to know where the corn and beans he eats come from, he follows Selu Tvya and her basket to the storehouse. Peeking through the cracks, he witnesses an amazing scene. His grandmother rubs her right side, and corn pours into the basket. She rubs her left side, and beans pour into the basket. The young boy is horrified, convinced his grandmother is a witch and he must kill her.

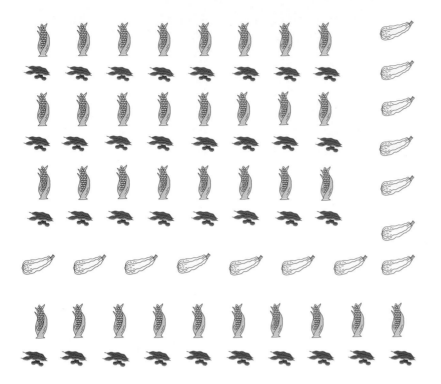

This diagram of Buffalo Bird Woman's garden shows her placement of the Three Sisters.

Upon returning to her dwelling, she notices the strange look on her grandson's face and guesses he has learned her secret. Her nose begins to bleed, and she interprets this as a sign of her impending death. She instructs her grandson on the disposition of her body. He is to clear some land and drag her body around it seven times. He attempts to do this, but is able to do this only twice, which was the beginning of the Cherokee custom of working the corn and beans only twice a season. As he dragged her body, wherever a drop of her blood fell on his right side, a corn plant sprang up. If on his left, a bean plant emerged. This is the origin of the Cherokee custom of planting corn and beans together.

The Seneca also have a myth with the image of these and other sustaining plants emerging from a woman's body. In their creation story, a woman falls (or is pushed) to earth from a hole in the sky. She later has a daughter who dies giving birth to the twins Good Mind and Evil Mind. Her daughter is buried and from her fingers grow bean plants, from her abdomen grows squash, and from her breasts, corn. Her feet produce potatoes and a spot above her forehead, tobacco.

In the Southwest in late winter, the Hopi observe Powamu, the nine-day Bean Dance sequence. As part of this ritual, *masi hatiqo*, gray limas saved by Hopis for innumerable generations, are sprouted. The trimmed sprouts and whole corn are cooked in a broth that is eaten as a ceremonial meal. Bean sprouts are also served to men in the community who have been observing a fast, abstaining from meat and salt as part of the spiritual rites. In addition, gray limas are planted in sand basins within the ceremonial space of the kiva, and their growth is believed to predict the productivity of the coming season.

A GALLERY OF BEANS

During the last decade, an increasing number of cooks and gardeners have discovered the rich lode of dried beans, peas, chickpeas, and *dals*. Since these legumes have been valued throughout the world for many thousands of years, they have rich and varied histories. Although our interest may focus on cooking them, dried legumes are so versatile that they furnish the basic material for hundreds of additional uses, ranging from sprouts to flour to printing ink.

Because of their size, ease of growing and harvest, self-pollination, beauty, and good storage qualities, beans and peas have often been saved and passed around to family members, neighbors, or friends for replanting. These open-pollinated (nonhybrid) varieties that predate 1940 are called heirloom varieties.

The heirloom varieties that are available to us today can usually be traced back to the dedicated efforts of a particular family or individual, such as John Withee of Massachusetts, who grew out 900 varieties of beans, or Ralph Stevenson, "the Bean King of Michigan," who regularly grew out 250.

COMMON BEANS
(Phaseolus vulgaris)
Kidney beans, black turtle beans, Great Northerns, pintos, cannellini beans—these beans are all of the same family and their varieties number over a thousand. Among these numbers we often find poetic and evocative names, such as 'Cherokee Trail of Tears', 'Wren's Egg', 'Black Valentine', 'Tongues of Fire', '1500 Year Old Cave Bean', and 'Lazy Wife'. Many have the names of native tribes attached to

them, and others have the names of early settlers. To plant and grow this commonplace legume is to link yourself directly and tangibly to the history of this country.

The common bean was thought to have originated in Peru. However, a recent analysis of similarities in protein between wild and domesticated beans points to two independent origins: Mexico and the southern Andes of Peru. Previous radiocarbon dating material from these two areas suggested that the beans from Peru were around 8,000 years old and those from Mexico were 7,000 years old. However, recent work with accelerated mass spectrometry, a more accurate dating method, has revealed beans from both areas to be approximately 5,000 years younger than originally thought.

From left to right, common beans: 'Bert Goodwin's', 'Miss Hamilton', and 'Wren's Egg'. (Photo by David Cavagnaro.)

In Italy, common beans became so popular in Tuscany that the nickname for Tuscans became *mangafagioli*, or the bean eaters. The origin of this name dates back to 1528 when some common beans from the New World were sent to Pope Clement VII, who in turn sent some on to Canon Pietro Valeriano in Florence. The canon grew them, had them cooked, tasted them, and approved. But more important, Alessandro de Medici, the head of Tuscany's ruling family, approved. Thus began the widespread cultivation of *Phaseolus vulgaris* in Tuscany.

LIMA BEANS
(Phaseolus lunatus)

The name of this bean is an English mispronunciation of Lima, the capital of Peru, which in turn was a Spanish corruption of the Quechua Indian word Rimac, the name for the river running through Lima. The Spaniards distributed limas from Lima to their colonies in the East Indies, Madagascar, and Africa, where the beans continue to be an important staple.

To many Americans, limas are the pale green things that spill out of a frozen square package. Inhabitants of the warm regions know better. In the South, where limas are traditionally called "butter beans" or "butter peas," mottled varieties, such as 'Florida Speckled', 'Jackson Wonder', and the red and white 'Christmas', reveal a part of the lima family that is colorful and likes to dress in plaids and stripes. The names of many of the heirloom varieties of the Southwest indicate not only their colors, but also their Native American origins: 'Hopi Orange', 'Cliff Dweller', 'Pima Beige', and 'Calico India Lima'.

Lima beans are categorized as large seeded or small seeded (known as sievas) and as bush beans or pole beans. Like common beans, limas are believed to have been domesticated in two separate areas of Mexico and Peru.

A small word of caution about lima beans: Do not consume large amounts of them raw or sprouted. In their chemical makeup, some contain a small amount of toxic cyanogens; the cyanogens are destroyed by the simple act of boiling.

RUNNER BEANS
(Phaseolus coccineus)

As the Mae West of the bean world, runner beans are big, showy, and gorgeous. In fact, there is a variety called 'Painted Lady' that sports scarlet and white bicolored blossoms. The better known 'Scarlet Runner' is an all-around beauty with red-orange flowers and lavender seeds veined with black. Other attractive beans include a chestnut-brown, a glossy black, and a white bean with white blossoms. Runner bean blossoms attract hummingbirds, who add their own glittery brilliance to the garden as they zip from flower to flower.

The runner bean originated in Mexico, where it was developed and cultivated by indigenous farmers. Pods of this bean that may be as old

From left to right, pole limas: 'Willow Leaf White', 'Red Calico', and 'Black'. (Photo by David Cavagnaro.)

as 6,000 years have been found in caves in Tamaulipas in northeastern Mexico, but botanists disagree over whether they were cultivated or wild. A wild small-seeded ancestor can still be found in Mexico and in Guatemala, clambering over vegetation in cool, partially shaded places. In addition to its value as food, for centuries these beautiful beans have had ceremonial and ornamental uses among native cultures of the Southwest and Mexico.

Although runner beans are most common as rapidly growing pole beans, there are bush versions. 'Gulliver'

grows to a mere 12 in. tall, while 'Hammond's Dwarf' and 'Dwarf Bees' are about 18 in. tall. All have scarlet blossoms. 'Aztec Dwarf White', an ancient variety, is a half-runner and grows to about 3 ft.

There are numerous varieties of runner bean seeds available. The Seed Savers Exchange's *Garden Seed Inventory, Fourth Edition*, a roster of all nonhybrid vegetable seeds available by catalog in the United States and Canada, lists 33 different runner bean varieties. Like common beans, there are varieties that flourish in the hot and dry conditions

From left to right, runner beans: 'Dutch White', 'Chestnut', and 'Jumbo Pinto'. (Photo by David Cavagnaro.)

of the Southwest and those that grow well in the cooler, shorter summers of the North.

TEPARY BEANS
(*Phaseolus acutifolius*)

Although not a familiar bean to most people, tepary beans may become better known in the future. Drought, increased energy costs to pump water in arid regions, and increasing desertification are all worldwide problems challenging the production of enough food for an ever-increasing population. Because of the tepary bean's ability to produce a high-protein crop under desert conditions, there has been increased interest in it by agriculturists looking for crops adapted to environmental stress. Plant breeders are also investigating the tepary's genetic material as a way to improve the common bean's drought resistance.

Tepary beans are native to Mexico and have been grown for at least 1,000 years by Native Americans living in the Sonoran desert area of Arizona. They are are specifically adapted to growing under extreme heat and dryness. Their roots grow twice as deep in the same amount of time as those of common beans, which enables them to tap deep reservoirs of soil moisture left by summer rains when upper levels of soil have dried out. And like the desert ephemerals that they are, tepary beans grow, flower, and set seed rapidly, before the moisture gives out and the drought sets in.

For the Papago Indians of the Southwest who have preserved and grown tepary beans for generations, this remarkable bean has special significance. There are growing songs sung for it, and the Indians associate a bountiful harvest of white tepary beans with the Milky Way—a scattered abundance across the night sky.

LENTILS
(*Lens culinaris*)

Cruise the bean aisle at the supermarket and there among the earth-toned hues one patch of salmon-orange always stands out—lentils, hulled and split, glowing like a lurid sunset. In this form, they are labeled *masoor dal* or red lentils, and they are an example of how confusing lentil terminology can be. In areas of the world under the influence of European cuisine, lentils are known in their whole, brownish green form or in the tiny black pellets also known as French lentils. However, in India and regions of the Near East, lentils are hulled and split, which make them easier to digest and faster to cook. Their interiors are yellow or salmon-orange.

Lentils are one of the most ancient plants cultivated by humans. They are associated with the beginnings of Neolithic agriculture and the attendant domestication of wheat and barley in the Near East. Carbonized lentils have been found in several villages in that region and have been dated to 7,000 B.C., but analysis of these seeds indicates they weren't wild but rather cultivated seeds that had been going through a process of domestication for a long time.

As Neolithic agriculture spread to Europe, western Asia, and the Nile valley, so did lentils. They have been found in royal tombs in Egypt dating from 2,200 B.C., but perhaps their most well-known role in history comes from the biblical Old Testament story of Jacob and Esau. According to the book of Genesis, Esau sold his birthright to his brother Jacob for a dish of pottage, which translates to a bowl of cooked lentils.

From left to right, tepary beans: 'Blue Speckled', 'White Secator', 'Black', and 'Brown Secator'. (Photo by David Cavagnaro.)

From left to right, lentils: 'Pardina', masoor dal, *and tiny black lentils. (Photo by David Cavagnaro.)*

From left to right, peas: 'Yellow Split', 'Raisin Capucinjer', and 'Green Split'. (Photo by David Cavagnaro.)

Today, the most common source of dried peas is no doubt the supermarket, where you can find packages of smooth green peas or yellow split peas, generally used for soup. But if you're going to grow your own, there are some interesting choices available. Several old European varieties have fragrant, bicolored red and pink or maroon and white flowers that can produce purple pods and peas that cook into a rich brown gravy. Some of these varieties have "Capuchin" in their names, which refers to the monastic order of that name. It is not known if this is a reference to the particular pea being preserved by a Capuchin monastery or to the resemblance of the pea blossom to the cowls of the monks.

Lentils are borne in tiny pods, with only one or two to a pod, and the plants resemble alfalfa, a close relative. Although the world's major lentil-growing regions are India and Turkey, it is also an important crop in dry regions of Canada and in the northwestern United States.

DRIED PEAS
(*Pisum sativum*)

From the archaic verse "Pease porridge hot, Pease porridge cold...," we get an idea of the original importance of peas. The peas of the verse were not the fresh, sweet delicacy that we so eagerly await in the spring. They were a more starchy pea that could be dried and stored against famine and the barren days of winter. This pea has been grown many more centuries than sweet green peas, which were the result of early breeding experiments and have been around only since the seventeenth century.

Peas are believed to have originated in western Asia. They have been found in deposits in central Turkey dated to 5,700 B.C. In the New World, the first peas were planted in 1494 at La Isabela, the ill-fated settlement on Hispaniola established by Christopher Columbus on his second voyage. Apparently, the peas fared better than the colonizers because by 1602 they were found growing in native villages in Florida.

FAVA BEANS
(*Vicia faba*)

Sturdy and robust, favas are hearty fare. Known as broad beans in England and *fèves* in France, favas, the beans' Italian name, has been adopted in this country.

Cave excavations in Sicily show that fava beans were being cultivated in 4,800 B.C. However, the earliest domestication of these historic beans is believed to have taken place much earlier in what is now Egypt. By the Iron Age in Britain, which roughly spanned the 700 years before the birth of Christ, the cultivation of these beans as stored provisions for humans and for forage for domesticated animals was widespread.

Favas are the hardiest of the bean tribe and stand alone in their preference for cool weather. Their size ranges from a compact 12-in. dwarf ('The Sutton') to an impressive 6-ft. plant ('Banner'), and they possess an earnest and diligent stiffness. Some varieties, as if to belie this proletarian appearance, will surprise you with very snappy looking black and white flowers. These flowers later produce rather rumpled and irregular dried beans that are deep tan, green, purple, or pale beige.

Most written material on favas contains a warning that some people of Mediterranean descent may be subject to an allergic reaction triggered by eating this bean. This condition—favism—is an anemia and is caused by a genetic disorder that results in a missing enzyme. When oxidative agents such as fava

From left to right, chickpeas: 'Black Kabuli', chana dal, and 'Garbanzo'. (Photo by David Cavagnaro.)

From top to bottom, favas: 'Suprifin', 'Guatemalan Purple', and 'Tarahumara'. (Photo by David Cavagnaro.)

bean alkaloids are consumed by people with this condition, the anemia is aggravated.

CHICKPEAS
(Cicer arietinum)

In the mid '70s, hummus, the tasty dip of puréed chickpeas, began to give new meaning to the word ubiquitous. As its popularity spread, hummus appeared at potluck dinners, delicatessens, picnics, and cocktail parties. Twenty years later, hardly anyone calls it "humus" anymore.

Known as garbanzo in Spanish and *ceci* in Italian, the English name for these nut-flavored legumes has nothing to do with chickens. The "chick" in chickpea is a corruption of *cicer*, its original name in Latin.

From left to right, Southern peas: 'Black-eyed', 'Mississippi Silver', and 'Pinkeye Purple Hull'. (Photo by David Cavagnaro.)

Chickpeas are one of the world's oldest cultivated crops. They are thought to have been originally domesticated at the eastern end of the Mediterranean around 7,500 B.C. Through thousands of years of selection, two main types emerged: the Kabuli and the Desi. The Kabuli type is distinguished by its familiar round shape and is what we generally think of when we think of a chickpea. It is widely available in its familiar beige form and is ground into flour used in the Mediterranean region and in India. There is also a smaller black variety available in Indian markets and to home gardeners. The Desi type has a ram's head shape and is usually found hulled and split under the name *channa dal*. Like lentils, chickpeas come only one or two per pod and grow on alfalfa-like plants.

SOUTHERN PEAS
(*Vigna unguiculata*; black-eyed peas, subs. *unguiculata*)
These earthy beans are so characteristic of the American South that some people assume they sprang fully formed from the red clay soil of Dixie. However, like the pigeon peas of the Caribbean, they came from Africa with the slave trade. Southern peas are thought to have first been cultivated in Ethiopia around 4,000 B.C. to 3,000 B.C. They remain an important crop in Africa, where the seeds, sprouts, and leaves are eaten.

The term "Southern pea" covers a rather confusing group: cowpeas, field peas, black-eyed peas, crowder peas, and cream peas. Methods of classification vary, ranging from seed type to culinary characteristics. Here is a general guide. Cowpeas and field peas are generic terms that refer to this culinary bean's additional use as animal fodder and soil enrichment. Plump black-eyed peas (most of which come from California) have a black spot at the hilum, the little scar where they are attached to the pod. Crowder peas are crowded together in the pod and have a square shape. Cream peas get their name from their color.

The South is known for its rich and colorful language, which can be found in the names of some Southern peas like 'Banquet Cream', 'Big Boy', 'Dixie Lee', 'Knuckle-hull Purple', 'Mississippi Silver', 'Big Red Ripper', 'Whippoorwill', and 'Zipper Cream'. Southern peas grow as vines, as bushes, or prostrate. The pods are long and thin, grow from 7 in. to 13 in., and can contain as many as 20 peas.

From left to right, pigeon peas: whole and toor dal (hulled and split). (Photo by David Cavagnaro.)

From left to right, soybeans: 'Lammer's Black', 'Envy', and 'Maple Arrow'. (Photo by David Cavagnaro.)

PIGEON PEAS
(Cajanus cajan)

If you're eating pigeon peas not far from where they're grown, you're in a warm place. Most pigeon peas are grown in India, but they are also an important crop in the Caribbean, Malawi, Uganda, and southeast Asia. They are short-lived perennial shrubs, growing to a height of 9 ft. The mature stems are often cut down and used as firewood after the pods have been harvested.

The earliest evidence for the cultivation of pigeon peas is uncertain. Most botanists favor India as the country of origin because of the pigeon pea's prominence there. (India currently produces 95% of the world's crop.) Other botanists suggest northern Africa because some 4,000-year-old fossilized remains found there are thought to be pigeon peas. With the African slave trade, pigeon peas reached the Caribbean, where on some islands they are still called congo peas or *pois angola*. Other Caribbean names include *gungo* or *gunga* peas, and, on the Spanish-speaking islands, *gandules*.

In India, hulled and split pigeon peas are known as *toovar dal, toor dal, or arhar dal*, and they are an important culinary staple. This *dal* is sometimes found in an oil-coated form; if that's the case, it should be rinsed in several changes of hot water before use.

SOYBEANS
(Glycine max)

All beans are choice morsels, but soybeans hold exalted rank. They are the most widely consumed legume on earth, which means that economically they are the most important bean in the world. In the form of "soybean futures," they are found in investment firms and in the

From left to right, mung beans: split *moong dal* and whole. *(Photo by David Cavagnaro.)*

Although we generally think of soybeans as a commercial or processed item, there are a number of varieties available for the home gardener. Breeding efforts have resulted in early bearers for eating in the green shell stage, such as 'Envy' and 'Butterbeans', and for use as a dried bean in short-season areas, such as the black-seeded 'Black Jet'. These plump egg-shaped beans also come in brown, red, yellow, and green and generally grow three to a pod on slightly fuzzed plants that are 1 ft. to 3 ft. high.

MUNG BEANS
(Vigna radiata)
As the runner-up to soybeans in versatility, these small olive-green beans are probably most familiar in their sprouted form, which is how they are found in many Chinese dishes. Mung beans are also the basis of the cellophane noodle used in Asian cuisines. Hulled and split, they reveal their creamy yellow interiors and in India are called *moong dal*. They are used in many cooked dishes, salads, and pancakes. A further example of their chameleon-like adaptability is their use in Thailand as a sweetened paste filling for pastries.

financial pages of newspapers in Tokyo, London, New York, and Chicago. The United States (followed by Brazil) is the largest producer, annually growing about 50% of the world's supply.

Soybeans are thought to have first been domesticated in northeastern China around 1,100 B.C. Today they are cultivated worldwide, but their use diverges significantly between East and West. In the Far East, they are an important food for humans. In the West, they are mostly processed into oil, plastics, paint, and adhesives, and the crushed residue is fed to animals. In this country, food-industry chemists have figured out how to spin soy

protein into textured vegetable protein (TVP), which can be flavored to imitate various meats and used as a meat substitute. Did you want that soyburger medium or well-done?

In addition to their rank as top bean in economic importance, soybeans rank as top bean in protein content and transmutability. Soy sauce, tofu, miso, soy milk, flour, fermented black beans, sprouts, oil, tempeh, and a sweetened bean paste are just some of the foods derived from this bean.

Azuki beans. (Photo by David Cavagnaro.)

From left to right, black grams: whole and urad dal *(hulled and split). (Photo by David Cavagnaro.)*

Archeological evidence suggests that mung beans were first domesticated in India at least 3,500 years ago and soon spread into other areas of Asia and into northern Africa. Although they are grown primarily for dried beans, their pods and immature seeds are also used as a vegetable. Like favas, mung beans are also used as a forage crop for livestock.

AZUKI BEANS
(Vigna angularis)
Azuki beans are a satiny burnt sienna color with a tiny streak of white and resemble small beads, like their mung and black gram relatives. In this country,

they are also known as adzuki and aduki, but phonetically azuki is correct.

These beans are a popular and important staple in Japan, where they are most commonly made into the sweetened red bean paste that is an ingredient in many confections. They are also eaten fresh and dried, and they are traditionally used in dishes for festive and celebratory occasions.

BLACK GRAMS
(Vigna mungo)
In a vivid description, the great horticulturist Liberty Hyde Bailey wrote in 1910 that this sprawling 2-ft. plant had "furrowed stems densely clothed with long brown

hairs" and yellowish flowers on the end of a "stout, hairy peduncle." These tiny oblong beans (usually about ⅜ in. long) come 10 to 15 to a pod, and it's a hairy pod you can be sure.

Black grams are a staple in Indian cooking. They are popular in northern India cooked whole and throughout the entire country in their hulled and split form, *urad dal*. In southern India, fried or roasted *urad dal* is used as a seasoning, imparting a nutlike flavor. Like its close relative the mung bean, *urad dal* is ground into a flour and used in the papery crisp wafers of *pappadums*.

BUYING AND STORING

Dried legumes are everywhere, and shell beans have become a sought-after summer delight. The increasing popularity of both is demonstrated by the ever-widening array available to cooks and gardeners. Both dried and frozen beans are easy to store, which means that they can be available year round at a moment's notice.

BUYING

Many supermarkets carry dried beans in bulk, as well as in packages, which are usually in 1-lb. sizes. Those stores with international sections are a good source for *dals*, pigeon peas, and fava beans. Whole-food and gourmet markets usually stock a wide variety of both conventionally and organically grown dried legumes. If the beans you want are not available locally, there are mail-order sources that offer an astonishing range of high-quality beans (see Sources on p. 165).

When buying dried beans, look for whole, uniform-size beans. Broken or split beans cook unevenly. Because their skin color fades with age, a rich color indicates a recent harvest. If you order beans through the mail, the mail-order company will do the sorting for you.

If you can find fresh shell beans at a market, look at the pods to determine the quality. They should be lumpy, suggesting the plump beans within, and rather leathery but not withered and dried out, which would indicate that they are not freshly harvested. Avoid pods with any sign of decay or mildew.

STORING

Dried beans can be stored for a long time, but not indefinitely. As they age, they continue to lose moisture, becoming drier and harder. This loss of moisture increases a bean's cooking time and decreases its flavor, so try to use beans within six months. Because the cooking time is influenced by the bean's age, avoid mixing beans of different ages in the same container.

Dried beans should be stored in a cool, dry place, ideally in airtight containers. Because of dried beans' attractiveness, many cooks like to store them in clear-glass mason jars on open shelves or on counters. If you follow this practice, make sure that the jars are not subject to heat from the stove or to fading from direct sunlight.

This bowl is full of a mix of the green-shelled pole beans 'Brockton' and 'Purple', along with pole limas 'Black', 'Winfield', and 'Cliff Dweller'. (Photo by David Cavagnaro.)

Shell beans in their pods will keep in the refrigerator for up to a week. Store them in an open plastic bag to maintain moisture, as well as some air circulation to prevent mold. Once they're shelled, they can be kept a day or two in an airtight container.

Cooked dried and shell beans will keep in the refrigerator for four or five days.

FREEZING

Beans may be frozen for storage at any stage. When soaking or cooking them, it pays to prepare extra and freeze them for future use. Then when you need beans, simply remove them from the freezer in the morning to thaw for dinner, or thaw them in a microwave on a defrost cycle. The amount of time will depend on the amount of beans.

Shell beans are one of the simplest foods to freeze, as well as one of the most successful. Remove them from their pods, pack them into airtight containers, and place them in the freezer. When they are thawed and cooked, they will maintain their shape for baking, simmering, or braising.

If you are cooking beans specifically for freezing, undercook them slightly to ensure that they maintain their shape and texture after thawing and reheating. Cooked beans will keep well in the freezer for two to three months.

GROWING AND HARVESTING

Gardening is a continuing education. As a cook whose menus revolve around what's in the garden, each year I like to experiment with new vegetables and varieties. This means that from late February through autumn I plant seeds, hundreds and hundreds of them, amazing miniature packets that encapsulate the mundane with the miraculous. Of all the seeds that I plant, those of the bean give me the most pleasure. They are unlike the tiny, dun-colored seeds of most other vegetables. Beans are seeds you can hold in your hand. Their ovalness and lustrous finish make them gratifying to the touch. Their size, shape, and color stand out against the dark of the receiving soil, a visible sign of your labors. The hard-working gardener can stand at the end of a row of just-sown beans and feel a swell of satisfaction at this evidence of industry, thrift, faith, hope, and any number of other virtues dear to inhabitants of the Land of the Protestant Work Ethic.

GETTING A GOOD START

Any discussion of growing begins with soil. "Feed the soil, not the plant" is a maxim of organic gardeners. Giving the soil a dose of granulated 5-10-5 fertilizer at the beginning of the growing season does not fit this maxim. Feeding the soil is the periodic addition of organic material, such as compost, manure, or cover crops (often called "green manure"). This organic matter is broken down by benefi-cial organisms in the soil, creating a fertile medium for growing healthy vegetables of superior taste and texture.

A second principle in growing healthy plants is crop rotation. Many disease and insect problems are carried in the soil. Growing varieties from the same family of plants in one place year after year encourages a buildup of these problems. Vegetable plants also vary in the amount and type of soil nutrients that they use up. It therefore makes sense to alternate plantings from year to year. (Eliot Coleman provides a full description of this important principle in the *The New Organic Grower.*) As contributors of nitrogen, legumes are a vital part of any rotation plan.

Emerging bean plants grow best in warm, well-drained soil that is rich in organic matter. (Photo by David Cavagnaro.)

Bean growers should take precautions not to work around their plants after watering them, after it rains, or when they are still wet with dew. Diseases such as anthracnose, bacterial blight, and rusts can be spread by wet leaves. Diseases and insects can also overwinter on plant debris, so it is good gardening practice at the end of the season to gather up dead plants and leaves and dispose of them, composting them only if the plants are healthy or if the compost heap will heat up enough to kill these organisms.

ADDING INOCULANTS

The ideal soil for legumes is high in organic matter, slightly acidic (a pH of 6 to 7), well drained (they do not like wet feet), not excessively nitrogenous, and located in full sun. However, unlike demanding vegetables like cauliflower or celery, legumes will produce under less-than-ideal conditions.

Soil moisture is important to legumes. From the time of planting until the seedlings' emergence, the soil should not be allowed to dry out. Later on, during flowering and pod formation, adequate water is again important, as stress can cause uneven formation of beans. The application of a mulch when the soil has warmed up is a good way to conserve moisture.

If germination of beans and peas is spotty, I've had good luck filling in the gaps by transplanting seedlings from a thicker stand. I make sure that the plants are less than 4 in. high and that the roots are disturbed as little as possible and encased in plenty of moist soil.

Growing beans and peas will always benefit the soil. This is because of a symbiotic relationship between them and a soil bacteria that results in the fixation of nitrogen nodules on leguminous roots. The soil bacteria, rhizobia, provide the legumes with access to nitrogen in the air, and the legume roots provide nourishment for the rhizobia colonies. These colonies, which are high in nitrogen, form nodules on the roots. As the bacteria dies, this nitrogen is released into the soil.

Dried on the vine, these beans are ready to harvest. (Photo by David Cavagnaro.)

Often planting instructions for peas and beans suggest treating them with an inoculant. For home gardeners, this inoculant usually comes in the form of a black dust, a combination of milled peat and a powdered culture of nitrogen-forming rhizobial bacteria. It's available through seed catalogs or garden supply stores.

For an inoculant to be effective, the correct strain of rhizobia must be matched to the legume. There are strains available for a pea and common bean combination, for fava beans, and for soybeans.

These products carry an annual expiration date and should be used fresh to ensure viability.

In garden soils that have been amended with organic material, an inoculant is not necessary because these soils usually contain enough minerals for legumes to form nitrogen. If a legume can get enough nitrogen from mineral sources, it will not make the effort to form nodules, even if the rhizobia bacteria are present in the soil. However, using a specific inoculant can increase yield and is strongly advised for soils low in organic matter or fertility, soils that haven't been gardened for a number of years, or soils where a particular legume has not been grown before.

To apply an inoculant, dig a furrow for the seeds, sprinkle a band of inoculant along the bottom, and plant the seeds in the furrow. This enables the roots to come into contact with the inoculant as they germinate. An alternate method is to moisten the seeds, place some inoculant in a bowl, roll the seeds around in it, and then plant.

HARVESTING DRY BEANS AND PEAS

Just as planting out plump and solid bean seeds into sun-warmed earth is a satisfying spring ritual, their autumn harvest is a rewarding closure to the horticultural cycle of germination and growth. Dried beans are quite tolerant when it comes to their harvest and can be picked over time. However, sustained wet or dry periods can cause the pods to drop off or open and, in a familiar phrase, spill the beans.

In a dry autumn, beans should be harvested as soon as the pods are brittle. If autumn rains are typical in your area, beans may have to be harvested before this stage. If so, bushes can be clipped off or yanked up and stacked off the ground and under cover, where they can dry until they're brittle. Pole beans can be clipped off at their base, disentangled, or yanked off their supports and stored the same way until they're brittle. If twine is used as support, it can be snipped at the top and bottom to simplify the removal of the plants.

Another method is to snip or pull individual pods from the plants and store them in open paper bags under cover. I prefer this procedure, as it makes threshing and cleaning easier, and the paper bags can be easily labeled with the name of the bean inside.

There are two basic methods to get the dry beans or peas out of their pods: hand shelling and threshing. When you have a small amount of beans, hand shelling this garden bounty can be a pleasant shared or solitary activity. For larger amounts, threshing is the way to go.

My favorite threshing method uses a feed sack or an old pillowcase and is best done outdoors or in an easily swept garage or cellar. Cut off one corner of the sack so the hole is large enough for the beans to pour through but small enough to block large bits of plants and pods. Tie this corner closed with twine or a large twist-tie, and stuff the dried plants or pods into the open end. Fold the sack over once and fasten it with clothespins or large safety pins. Throw it on the ground and turn on the radio. Find something with a good beat, jump on that sack, and start dancing. Basic steps in this dance are the "left-right hop" and the "flat-foot slide."

If the dried bean pods are removed from the plants, it makes threshing and winnowing easier. These beans are 'Mitla Black', grown for at least 800 years by the Mitla Indians in Oaxaca, Mexico. (Photo by David Cavagnaro.)

When it feels like all of the beans have been released, briefly crunch the contents further with your hands to break open any closed pods, and give the bag a couple of shakes to direct all the beans into the tied corner. Hold this corner over a deep basket, plastic bucket, or cardboard peck container, and untie it, releasing the beans into the container.

Dried pods can also be dumped on a tarp and danced on. Or, for those who don't dance, dried pods can be jogged on or beaten with a flail. (A flail is a traditional threshing device made of a wooden staff with a shorter, free-swinging stick attached to one end.) Lacking a flail, I have had success using a scrap of white PVC pipe with a 1½-in. diameter.

Or you can use food and garden writer Diane Bilderbeck's method. She turns to her clothes dryer. Pour the dry bean pods into a pillowcase and tie the end shut. Place the pillowcase in the dryer with a couple of sneakers to break up the pods. Set the temperature gauge for low heat and dry for 30 minutes, or until the pods are broken open. Remove the pillowcase from the dryer and step on it to release the beans. Give it a few shakes so that when it is opened the beans will be at the bottom, the pod debris at the top. Pour the beans into a container.

The next step is an ancient process called winnowing. This is the separation of the

A broad-bottomed basket can help in separating beans from large pieces of chaff. (Photo by David Cavagnaro.)

beans or peas from the chaff, as fine bits of dried plant debris are called. Winnowing is best done outside on a breezy day. If breezes don't come your way, you can make your own with an electric fan or blower from a vacuum cleaner.

The first step is to shake the beans back and forth in their container so that larger pieces of debris rise to the surface (see the photo at left). Remove as much of the debris as possible. The beans are then poured slowly from high in the air into a deep basket or plastic bucket so the breeze can carry the chaff away. You will need to repeat this pouring several times until the beans are clean. Due to the vagaries of a stiff breeze and bouncing beans, there will be some that escape their container. Using a tarp or old sheet underneath the container, weighted down at the corners, is a good idea so that stray beans can be easily retrieved.

SAVING SEED
The seed that a gardener holds in hand at planting time is a living link in a chain stretching back to our Neolithic past. This seed is the container of a vast amount of history, of genera-

tion after generation of our ancestors faithfully selecting seeds and growing them out, year after year. Whenever gardeners decide to save their own seeds, they become a part of this ancient chain.

The number of these traditional open-pollinated (non-hybrid) varieties available in the United States has declined drastically in the last 50 years (see the sidebar on the facing page). The factor most responsible for the severe decline of these seeds and related garden diversity has been the proliferation of hybrid seeds.

Hybrid seeds are produced by deliberately crossing two different parent varieties. There are definite advantages for seed companies selling hybrids. While somewhat more expensive to produce, they sell for more and thus are more profitable than open-pollinated seeds. Seed saved from hybrids for replanting is either sterile or reverts to its parentage, forcing farmers and gardeners to continually reorder. And to beat the competition, the parentage of a hybrid can be kept secret. For the home gardener, hybrid seed may produce more vigorous plants.

This array of bean seeds is a testimonial to the selection and preservation efforts of dedicated growers that have been taking place for over 2,000 years. (Photo by David Cavagnaro.)

GENETIC DIVERSITY

Today many botanists and agriculturists are alarmed at the steady decline in the numbers of open-pollinated seeds. Once the last seed of a variety loses its viability, that variety is gone forever. The disappearance of so many varieties erodes our genetic resources. A recent example of this erosion and of just how fragile our supplies are comes from the 1995 *Garden Seed Inventory, Fourth Edition*, which lists and describes all non-hybrid vegetable seeds available commercially in the United States and Canada. In 1981, 136 varieties of cabbage were offered by seed dealers. By 1994, that total had fallen to 75. Only 53 of the original 136 remained in that 75. Of the 75 varieties offered, 47 were being carried by just one or two dealers. Unless we have genetic diversity in our food crops, our food supply is vulnerable to epidemics such as the Irish potato famine of the 1840s or the U.S. corn blight of 1970.

Why should the home gardener save seed or buy open-pollinated and heirloom seeds? Taste, for one. As exemplars, I point to the luscious 'Brandywine' tomato, the tender and flavorful 'Early Jersey Wakefield' cabbage, and the gratifyingly delicious 'Jenny Lind' melon. Another reason is performance. With generations of home gardeners and small regional growers selecting seeds from plants that performed the best for them, many open-pollinated and heirloom varieties gradually developed resistances to local insect and disease problems and became adapted to soils and climate of specific areas.

This characteristic is especially true of beans, probably the easiest seeds to save from the vegetable garden.

Open-pollinated vegetable varieties often have an extended harvest period to accommodate the home gardener. Hybrids, because their main market is farmers producing on a huge scale, are bred to accommodate mechanical harvesting and usually mature all at once. Growing heirlooms and open-pollinated vegetables is an adventure—a foray into poetic metaphor, into history, and into unexpected and wondrous colors, forms, and

textures. Saving seeds continues the home gardener's adventure and furnishes the pleasure of participating in a vital agricultural ritual.

Bean-seed specifics

Without a doubt, beans are the vegetable that turns gardeners into seed savers. Beans are beautiful, like gifts from a plant, and they are easy to harvest and save.

Runner beans require insects to trip their self-pollinating mechanism. (Photo by David Cavagnaro.)

Generations of home gardeners have set aside common bean and pea seeds for next season.

Legume blossoms contain both male and female organs. They are self-pollinating, and fertilization usually takes place before the flower opens. For this reason, insect cross-pollination, although it does occasionally occur, is uncommon. The amount of cross-pollination depends on the type of blossom, the number of bees and other pollinating insects present, and the amount of other pollen and nectar sources available for these insects.

Because cross-pollination is so rare, home gardeners can generally save the seeds of common beans and peas and expect them to remain true to type. To lessen the possibility of cross-pollination, separate varieties by a tall crop or by 100 ft. To eliminate the possibility altogether, grow only one variety or use cages or the blossom-bagging method.

Runner beans, limas, favas, and peas have showy blossoms and are regularly visited by bees. Because of this, cross-pollination can occur within the species of this group; in other words, two different lima bean varieties may be crossed, but not a lima and a runner bean. To ensure purity, extra precautions must be taken in saving the seeds of this group.

There are two ways to do this without resorting to the recommended 100 ft. of separation between varieties. The first method is caging and is useful for bush varieties. Cages are easy to make. They are simply wooden frames covered securely with window screening or floating row covers. They need to be in place from the first to the last blossom.

The second method, blossom bagging, takes a bit more dedication. Using a floating row cover or a similar light-transmitting material, carefully isolate a raceme of flowers by surrounding it with the material and then tying the material securely. The blossom bag can be removed when tiny pods emerge from the flowers. As the bags are removed, tag the raceme in some way to identify it as seed to be saved.

Runner beans require an additional step. Because they need insects to trip their self-pollinating mechanism, the gardener must play bumble bee to ensure that there is no crossing between varieties. To simulate the insect's role, remove the blossom bag or cage (for dwarf varieties) and depress the bottom part of each new flower. Continue each day until the desired number of seed pods have been produced.

It is best to save seed only from healthy plants, as various diseases can be passed on through the seed.

Seed storage

When saving beans for seed, remember that the largest seeds will produce the most vigorous plants. Stored under cool, dry conditions, beans will remain viable for years. However, with each year, their germination rates drop. The greatest enemies of stored seeds are heat and moisture. For planting out next season, bean seeds can be stored in envelopes or bags in a cool, dry cabinet. For long-term storage, an airtight glass or metal container should be used.

Legume seeds are susceptible to damage from bean weevils. These insects lay eggs in the young pods. When the larvae hatch, they feed on the bean seed, destroying saved seeds in a very short time. To prevent this, freeze bean seeds before storing them. Weevil eggs are killed by three days at 0°F, but the seeds should be left in the freezer for five days because all parts of a home freezer may not reach 0°F. If you're freezing beans in an airtight container, allow the container to sit out overnight to reach room temperature after you remove it from the freezer. If the container is opened too soon after removal, it will cause condensation to form on the beans, and they will take up moisture.

GROWTH HABITS

Among the vegetables we grow in our gardens, beans, and to some extent peas, are unusual in their growth characteristics. Like the comic strip characters Mutt and Jeff, they come in short and tall. The tall, climbing types are known as pole varieties; the short types are bush varieties. The ancestors of our common, lima, and runner beans are vines. Pole beans have retained this vining aspect, whereas bush beans are genetic dwarf varieties that have been selected through the centuries.

Pole beans

Pole beans and trellis-grown peas save garden space because they grow up, not out. A 10-ft. row of pole beans growing up 7-ft. bean poles has about the same leaf area as 30 ft. of bush beans. (It is leaf area exposed to sun that brings on the beans.) In my garden, this translates to the same yield from 4 ft. of trellised pole beans as I get from 12 ft. of bush beans. Pole beans are also easier to pick—no stooping. Because pole beans keep their pods up in the air away from ground moisture, they are a

Bean teepees can have more than one function. (Photo by David Cavagnaro.)

good crop in areas with heavy fall rains. And if you're interested in getting a long harvest season from one planting, these are your beans. Because they are indeterminate, pole beans will produce as long as you keep the pods picked.

The most familiar and probably the most widely used structure for growing pole beans is the traditional teepee (see the photo above). Its wide-based form makes it very stable, but there are several disadvan-

Pole beans grown on a twine trellis can easily be removed by snipping the twine at the top and bottom. (Photo by David Cavagnaro.)

tages. Pole beans are hefty vines and need ample space. In a teepee, there is no room at the top, causing congestion and resulting in a huge mass of tangled vegetation. It is also difficult to pick the beans inside the teepee unless it's big enough to include the picker.

There are many other structures to support pole beans, such as a trellis frame with nylon netting, wire fencing, or twine repeatedly zigzagged from top to bottom (see the

photo at left). Trellis frames can be constructed of wooden 2-in. by 2-in. stakes, sturdy saplings, metal fence posts, or white plastic PVC pipe. Circular aluminum and nylon twine supports are available through some seed catalogs. Poles can be wooden 2-in. by 2-in. stakes, sturdy saplings, or metal fence posts. Or you can simply use single 7-ft. bean poles spaced 2 ft. to 3 ft. apart. In England, runner beans are grown on a trellis made of sapling in the form of Xs located 4 ft. apart and lashed to a connecting staff at the center of the X. (See the illustrations on the facing page for examples of bean supports.)

You should set up structures for vining beans and peas before you plant because germinating seeds and young plants are brittle and vulnerable to injury. Whatever support you choose for pole beans, plan on a height of 6 ft. to 7 ft., or as high as you can comfortably reach. The total height of the support should be 8 ft. to 9 ft. because it needs to be firmly anchored in the ground. Pole beans grow vigorously, and toward the end of the season, a support fully loaded with

bean vines and pods needs to have a firm anchor.

To establish the support, sink the poles 1½ ft. to 2 ft. into the soil. The best way of doing this is to use a heavy iron digging bar (known in some circles as a "persuader") to drive the holes. Then stand on a sturdy stepladder and tap the poles in with a 2-lb. sledgehammer. Finally, firmly compact the soil around the pole, tamping with your feet or the rounded end of the digging bar.

If you're using nylon trellis netting, it should be supported vertically every 6 ft. Because of the weight of mature pod-bearing bean vines, some sort of horizontal support for the top of the netting is advisable.

Some pole bean plants are quite beautiful and make good candidates for growing over an arbor. I would put all runner beans in this category. They have profuse flowers at the end of 6-in. to 8-in. stems. Those with brilliant scarlet blossoms are showstoppers, but the pure white blooms of 'White Dutch' and the bicolor blooms of 'Painted Lady' are lovely. Some pole beans, such as

BEAN SUPPORTS

Double-frame trellis

Trellis netting between supports

X trellis

Commercially available bean tower

Bean pole

'Cherokee Trail of Tears' and 'Vermont Cranberry', produce mauve or rosy blooms with showy purple or maroon pods.

Corn plants may be used as bean poles, but for a successful bean crop, it is important to use the right corn varieties. The corn should be a tall variety, such as 'Hickory King' or 'Bloody Butcher', both of which grow at least 8 ft. high. It should be planted in hills 3 ft. or 4 ft. apart, with six seeds per hill. When the corn has germinated and is finger length, thin to the four healthiest and plant two or three bean seeds in the side of the hill. The beans should be shade-tolerant varieties adapted to growing on corn, such as 'Genuine Cornfield', 'Turkey Craw', or 'Ruth Bible'.

Bush beans

The most obvious advantage of bush beans is that you don't have to erect a support. Just drop the seeds in a furrow, cover them, dust off your hands, and walk away. Bush beans also bear earlier than pole beans, a useful trait in short-season areas and for those looking for the earliest green beans. They are determinate, bearing just one crop and then ceasing

Beans as beautiful as 'Davis Purple Pole' can be showcased on a decorative trellis. (Photo by David Cavagnaro.)

production, so for an extended harvest, you'll have to practice succession planting.

Bush beans are usually planted in rows 18 in. to 36 in. apart. When planning your row widths, keep access for harvesting and the size of mature plants in mind. In humid areas, row spacing should be 36 in., sufficient for good air circulation. Some gardeners prefer an intensive planting in which each seed is planted equidistant from its neighbors.

Although the garden image that bush beans enjoy is one

of tidiness, in reality they can be quite slovenly, draping themselves over adjacent plants and lounging around on your garden paths. This is particularly true of a group known as half-runners, or twining beans. Half-runners, such as 'White Aztec' or 'Bert Goodwin', generally attain a height of about 2 ft. but send out a few 3-ft. runners. To keep these plants in their rows and off the ground, you can use a restraint of stakes with a row of twine every 8 in. or so.

GROWING BEANS
Common beans

Seed depth: 1 in. to 1½ in., depending on the size of the seed (plant large seed deeper)

Soil temperature: minimum 65°F, optimum 70°F to 85°F

Seed spacing: *Bush:* Plant every 2 in., then thin to stand 4 in. to 6 in. apart in the row. For intensive bed planting, place seed every 5 in. *Pole:* Plant 6 to 8 seeds around each pole, with each seed 6 in. from the pole. Thin to the 3 best seedlings, with at least 6 in. between them. For rows with twine or netting supports, plant 3 in. apart, then thin to stand 6 in. apart. *Twining:* Plant 2 in. apart in rows, then thin to stand 4 in. to 6 in. apart.

Row spacing: *Bush*: 18 in. to 30 in.; *Pole*: 3 ft. to 4 ft.; *Twining*: 24 in. to 36 in.

Common beans require warm soil for successful germination. Many gardeners find it difficult to wait until the moment the soil has warmed sufficiently to keep their bean seeds from rotting and so have devised ways to nudge the season a little. For impatient gardeners, there are methods that can speed up the process (see the sidebar at right).

The snap-bean season can be extended by the successive planting of bush beans. Take your cue from the plants themselves and wait until the second level of leaves has formed before planting the next crop. Another method for extending the harvest is to sow an early crop of bush beans and, at the same time, plant pole beans for a main-season crop. Keep beans picked to encourage production.

Harvest: For green or snap beans, pods should be firm and fleshed out, and the seeds inside should be undeveloped or very small. For shell beans, harvest when the seeds are plump and fully formed but before they have

'Rattlesnake' pole beans.
(Photo by David Cavagnaro.)

started to dry out. The pod usually changes color, becomes more flexible, and starts to thin out. For dry beans, pods should get as dry as possible in the garden. When the plants have lost all their leaves and the pods are brittle, or before prolonged wet or wintry weather, pull the pods or the entire bush up to dry under cover, if necessary. Thresh and winnow or shell the beans by hand.

Lima beans
Seed depth: 1 in. to 1½ in., depending on the size of the seed (plant large seed deeper)
Soil temperature: 70°F minimum

FOR THE EARLIEST BEANS

- Start a batch of seed in 2-in. pots three weeks before the average date of the last frost. The seedlings will be ready to be hardened off and transplanted three weeks later. Cover them with a floating row cover when you transplant them.

- Prewarm the soil with black plastic for at least a week before planting.

- Sow the seeds in 6-in.- to 8-in.-high raised beds. The beds warm up faster in the spring, with soil temperatures as much as 4°F to 5°F higher than a standard bed.

- Plant darker bean seeds, which are more resistant to rotting in cool soil than light-colored beans.

- Take your chances with soaking the seed. One expert writes that it should never be done as it can crack or damage the seed structure. Another cautions to soak for only one hour and then plant, while a third advises the gardener to soak the bean seeds until they swell, place them in a single layer between two moist paper towels, enclose them in plastic to prevent evaporation, and keep them at 70°F to 80°F. If you do this, check daily for the radicle, or rudimentary root. When it first appears, plant the seeds carefully, firming the soil lightly.

Lima bean plant and pods. (Photo by Derek Fell.)

Seed spacing: *Bush*: Plant every 2 in., then thin to stand 4 in. to 8 in. apart in the row. For intensive bed planting, space seed every 6 in. to 8 in. *Pole*: Plant 6 to 8 seeds around each pole, with each seed 6 in. from the pole. Thin to the 3 best seedlings, with at least 6 in. between them. For rows with twine or netting supports, plant 3 in. apart, then thin to stand 6 in. apart.

Row spacing: *Bush*: 18 in. to 30 in.; *Pole*: 3 ft. to 4 ft.

The difference between fresh lima beans and frozen ones is analogous to that between summer-ripe tomatoes from your garden and those that you might buy at the supermarket in January. The succulence and nutlike flavor of fresh limas are so fine that, though out of their element in my central New York state garden, I cross my fingers and plunge ahead, growing them every year with varying degrees of success.

To produce a crop, limas need a long, warm growing season. This means that northern and cool-region gardeners should start their limas in 2-in. pots or grow a short-season bush type. To nudge the season along, you can use the tricks in the sidebar on p. 45.

Limas, especially the large-seeded pole varieties, bear over a long period and require more nutrients than common beans. They respond well to occasional applications of fertilizer during the growing season. Although limas are heat lovers, too much of a good thing can cause them to drop their blossoms. This may happen on sunny days when the temperature reaches 90°F, unless they are well watered.

When planting limas, look for a tiny scar on one side. This is the hilum, commonly known as the "eye," although belly button might be a more accurate term. This is where the bean was attached to its surrounding pod. When you plant, try to place the lima with the eye looking down-ward because the root emerges from the hilum.

Harvest: For shell beans, harvest when the seeds are plump and fully formed but before they have started to dry out. Because it's hard to feel the beans inside the pods, this stage can sometimes be difficult to ascertain. (These stiff pods also make shucking limas more time-consuming than peas or shell beans.) With pole limas, it helps to look at their pods when they are backlit on a sunny day. The translucency of the pod reveals the size of the beans inside. For dry beans, pods should get as dry as possible in the garden, but dry lima pods shatter easily if left out too long. When the plants have lost all their leaves, or before prolonged wet or wintry weather, pull the pods or the entire bush up to dry under cover, if necessary. Thresh and winnow or shell the beans by hand.

Runner beans

Seed depth: 1 in. to 1½ in., depending on the size of the seed (plant large seed deeper)

Soil temperature: 60°F minimum

Seed spacing: *Bush:* Plant every 2 in., then thin to stand 4 in. to 6 in. apart in the row. For intensive bed planting, space seed every 6 in. *Pole:* Plant 6 to 8 seeds around each pole, with each seed 6 in. from the pole. Thin to the 3 best seedlings, with at least 6 in. between them. For rows with twine or netting supports, plant 3 in. apart, then thin to stand 6 in. apart. *Twining:* Plant 2 in. apart in rows, then thin to stand 4 in. to 6 in. apart.

Row spacing: *Bush:* 2 ft.; *Pole:* 3 ft. to 4 ft.; *Twining:* 2 ft. to 3 ft.

Although a great admirer of their gorgeous blossoms, I sometimes think that as a culinary pleasure, runner beans have been hampered by their extraordinary beauty. Their best-known cultivar, 'Scarlet Runner', is usually found in the ornamental sections of seed catalogs, and it is in this guise that it is usually grown in this country.

Because they tolerate cooler soils and growing conditions, runner beans are a popular garden vegetable in England, where breeding efforts have produced many more varieties than the standard 'Scarlet Runner'. Although most familiar in their vining forms, there is a white-flowered half-runner 'Aztec Dwarf White' and a scarlet-flowered bush variety 'Hammond's Dwarf'.

Runner beans depend on insects (usually honeybees and bumblebees) to trip their self-pollinating mechanism, but their production is still on the shy side. Temperatures over 90°F may prevent pod set. For continual pod production, it's important to keep the pods picked, or the plants will cease flowering. Runner bean pods eventually attain stupendous size, growing 12 in. to 15 in. Pole varieties grow vigorously. They need strong supports and appreciate a mulch to conserve soil moisture.

Runner beans are perennial in warm regions and produce a tuberous root. In areas where the ground freezes, the roots may be dug in the fall, stored over the winter in moist sand, and replanted in the spring for an early start.

Harvest: You can harvest runner bean flowers for salads and stir-fries. For green or snap beans, harvest when the pods are young and tender and under 6 in. The pods should be firm and fleshed out, with the seeds inside undeveloped. For shell beans, harvest when the seeds are plump and fully formed but before they have started to dry out. The pod becomes more flexible and thinned out. For dry beans, pods should get as dry as possible in the garden. When the plants have lost all their leaves, or before prolonged wet or wintry weather, pull the pods or the entire bush up to dry under cover, if necessary. Thresh and winnow or shell the beans by hand.

Tepary beans

Seed depth: ½ in.

Soil temperature: 65°F

Seed spacing: *Twining:* Plant every 4 in.

Row spacing: 24 in. to 36 in.

Tepary beans are adapted to growing in arid regions under conditions that would stress other beans: intense heat, drought, and alkaline soils. Usually sown in double rows 6 in. apart, their planting in the Southwest is timed to coincide with seasonal rains. When grown in locations with high humidity and soil moisture, tepary beans grow well but eventually become infected with bean mosaic virus. They often carry this virus, which appears to be more damaging in moist climates, yet can be tolerated in arid regions.

Harvest: For dry beans, harvest when the plant has matured by pulling it up. Dry it for 4 to 7 days. Thresh and winnow or shell the beans by hand.

Fava beans
Seed depth: 1 in. to 3 in., depending on the soil (deeper in dry, sandy soil)
Soil temperature: 40°F
Seed spacing: *Bush*: Plant every 6 in. to 12 in. in rows. For intensive bed planting, space seed 8 in. to 12 in.
Row spacing: 18 in. to 36 in.

Fava plants are tough. Some varieties are hardy to 10°F, and all possess an aggressive taproot that can penetrate compacted soil. Their seeds sprout in very cool soil, and

they are the only bean that thrives in cool weather, growing best at 40°F to 70°F. Favas are also tolerant of most soils, growing well at a pH from 5.5 to 7.0, but preferring a pH of 6.0.

Although favas grow like an upright bush, their height ranges from 18 in. to 6 ft. Because they often need support, many gardeners plant them in a double row 6 in. to 12 in. apart, with seed spaced every 8 in. to 12 in. In windy areas or for tall varieties, added support from twine and stakes may be necessary.

Because of their hardiness, favas can be sown in early spring or in the fall and wintered over. In areas of mild winters with temperatures normally above 15°F, such as the Pacific coast, these beans can be planted in late October and November or very early in spring. In sections of the country with very cold winters (temperatures regularly below 10°F), the beans should be planted at the same time as peas, or even a bit earlier.

Fava blossoms lose viability at 85°F, so these beans are difficult to grow in areas of

early summer heat. Gardeners in these regions may want to try *ful medames*, the Egyptian fava, which is reputed to be the only heat-tolerant member of this cool-weather tribe.

Harvest: For greens, pinch off the leafy tips when the plants have 5 flower whorls. (As a bonus, this helps to control black aphids and stimulate additional growth.) Fava greens can be steamed like spinach or stir-fried. For delicious and very tender shell beans, harvest at ½ in. or smaller. Larger beans have a more obvious skin, which some cooks like to remove. For dry beans, harvest when pods blacken or begin to shrivel and dry up. If wet weather sets in during harvest season, pick the pods as they begin to shrivel, or when the hilum turns black. Shell and dry the beans in a well-ventilated area away from direct sunlight.

Peas
Seed depth: 1 in.
Soil temperature: minimum 40°F, optimum 50°F to 75°F
Seed spacing: *Bush*: Plant every 2 in. For intensive bed planting, space seed every 4 in. *Vine*: Plant every 2 in.
Row spacing: *Bush*: 12 in.; *Vine*: 30 in. to 36 in.

Glittering with early morning dew, pea vines are among the most beautiful plants in the vegetable garden. Some varieties such as 'Dwarf Gray Sugar' snow peas and most of the old varieties of dry soup peas have the added loveliness of red-violet blossoms.

Gardeners have a variety of peas to pick from: sugar snaps with crisp, succulent pods and peas; the more delicate flat-podded snow pea; shelling, or English, peas; and traditional soup peas. All of these are vines that range from 2 ft. to 6 ft. However, a few varieties, like 'Novella' and 'Lacy Lady', could be considered bush forms. These peas are short, semi-leafless plants that produce hundreds of threadlike tendrils. These tendrils form a dense network that is more or less self-supporting.

All peas are cool-weather crops. Although they will germinate at temperatures as low as 40°F, the cooler the soil, the slower the germination. If they sit in wet soil too long before sprouting, they will rot. Although the seeds are capable of germinating at 40°F, the minimum temperature for plant growth is 45°F. Once they're growing and spring days begin to heat

Fava bean blossoms. (Photo by Scott Vlaun.)

up, peas appreciate a mulch to keep their shallow roots cool and moist.

Peas will grow in a variety of soils as long as they are well drained and have a pH above 6.0. For best pod production, they need a good supply of phosphorus and potash, which can be supplied by adding wood ashes or limestone to the soil. If pods are maturing during hot weather, keep the plants' roots well watered and always pick at least every other day to encourage their production.

Although most successful as a spring crop, peas can be grown for a fall crop with varying degrees of success.

Choose a short-season variety and take steps to provide cool, moist soil conditions for germination. This can be done by planting an inch deeper than usual, by mulching, and by planting in 4-in.-wide trenches.

Short-vined peas, which produce the earliest harvests, can be planted in wide beds to grow without support or grown in a band the width of your hoe to climb up twine strung every 8 in. between 3-ft. stakes. They can also be planted to grow up "pea brush," any generously branched brush or prunings stuck in the ground as support for short-vined peas.

'Desiree Purple Pod' soup pea. (Photo by Susan Kahn.)

Tall vines, which generally produce more over a longer season, need a trellis. This can be nylon or metal trellising secured to poles, or it can be a frame of saplings or wooden 2-in. by 2-in. stakes with garden twine zigzagged between top and bottom. This system initially takes more effort, but at the end of the season, twine and vines are easily clipped off and composted.

Harvest: For greens, snip the terminal 3 in. to 4 in. of the pea vines for use in stir-fries or salads. For snowpeas, pinch off the pods when they are young, tender, and flat, before the peas inside develop. For sugarsnaps, pinch off the pods when they are crisp and plump. If any strings have developed, pinch almost through the tip of the pod with thumb and forefinger, grasp the pod, and pull it outward. The string should remain attached to the vine. For shelling peas, pick as soon as the pods are filled out and use or process them soon, as their sugar starts to convert to starch within several hours of harvest. For dry peas, allow them to dry completely on the vine. Either pick individually or pull the plants up when dry and crisp. Thresh and winnow or shell the peas by hand.

Chickpeas
Seed depth: 1 in.
Soil temperature: 65°F
Seed spacing: *Bush:* Plant every 2 in. to 3 in., then thin to stand 6 in. apart in the row. For intensive bed planting, space seed every 12 in.
Row spacing: 30 in. to 36 in.

Seed catalogs offer two varieties of chickpeas: the familiar beige type and a smaller, faster-maturing 'Kabuli', which produces black seeds. Each chickpea pod produces one or two seeds.

Chickpeas need a long, warm season and, like other legumes, require moist soil while germinating to produce strong plants. These lovely plants are quite drought resistant and can be grown in areas of low rainfall.

All surfaces of the chickpea plant are covered by tiny moist hairs (giving it a silvery appearance), which exude malic acid. Malic acid is similar to citric acid and is found in apples, grapes, and rhubarb. After contact with the plant, some people are bothered by a rash.

Harvest: For dry chickpeas, allow the plants and pods to dry completely. When the plants have lost all their leaves, or before prolonged wet or wintry weather, pull the plants up to dry under cover, if necessary. Thresh and winnow the chickpeas when the pods are dry and crisp.

Soybeans
Seed depth: 1 in.
Soil temperature: minimum 55°F, optimum 65°F to 85°F
Seed spacing: *Bush:* Plant every 3 in. to 6 in. in rows.

For intensive bed planting, space seed every 6 in.
Row spacing: 15 in. to 30 in.

In the last decade, seed catalogs have offered the home gardener a greater range of these high-protein beans. There are varieties that have been developed for eating as shell beans, such as 'Envy', 'Butterbeans', and 'Maple Arrow'. Handsome black ones with thin skins and fine flavor, such as 'Jet Black' and 'Lammer's Black', make excellent dry beans.

Harvest: For shell beans, harvest when the seeds are plump and fully formed but before they begin to dry out. The pod usually changes color, becomes more flexible, and starts to thin out. For dry beans, pods should get as dry as possible in the garden. When the plants have lost all their leaves, or before prolonged wet or wintry weather, pull the pods or the entire plants up to dry under cover, if necessary. Thresh and winnow or shell the beans by hand.

Southern peas
Seed depth: ½ in. to 1 in.
Soil temperature: 70°F
Seed spacing: *Bush:* Plant every 4 in. *Twining:* Plant every 4 in. *Prostrate:* Plant every 4 in.
Row spacing: 30 in. to 42 in.

Southern peas require a long warm season and are known for their ability to produce in marginal soils. Pods vary in size, ranging from 6 in. to a whopping 14 in.

Growth forms of Southern peas can be compact, vining, or prostrate. The vining type can be grown in rows spaced 30 in. apart and trained to a trellis down the middle. They lack twining tendrils so may need to be gently tied to a support. Prostrate plants need wide row spacing to accommodate their sprawl.

For northern gardeners, a breeding program at the University of Minnesota has produced Southern peas that germinate in cool soils (55°F to 60°F), produce compact plants, and mature quickly. Two of these varieties, 'Minnesota 13' and 'Minnesota 157', are available through Seeds Savers Exchange (see Sources on p. 166).

Harvest: For shell peas, harvest when the seeds are plump and fully formed, but before they have started to dry out. The pod becomes

'Butterbeans' soybean. (Photo by David Cavagnaro.)

more flexible and thinned out and changes from green to cream, yellow, red, purple, or brown, depending on the variety. For dry peas, pods should get as dry as possible in the garden. When the plants have lost all their leaves, or before prolonged wet or wintry weather, pull the pods or the entire plant up to dry under cover, if necessary. Thresh and winnow or shell the beans by hand.

FLATULENCE: FACT AND FARCE

"Beans, beans, the musical fruit. The more you eat, the more you toot." This bit of rhymed doggerel is undoubtedly familiar to every English-speaking schoolchild in the world. German children grow up with "Every bean sounds its note, every lentil its own phf-f-f-ft." Italians have defined a fart as the bean's soul ascending to heaven. These widespread aphorisms point to a fact that most of us are already familiar with: There is a connection between beans and flatulence.

Flatulence, the polite term for the passing of intestinal gas, or flatus, through the posterior exit, is a fact of life. Any person who eats and has a digestive system does this an average of 14 times a day. This gas is primarily carbon dioxide, with nitrogen, hydrogen, a bit of oxygen, and several sulphur-containing compounds. About one in three adults also produces methane, a flammable gas.

Flatulence is caused by sugars, starches, and fiber that reach the large intestine without being digested. In legumes, the offending ingredients are certain oligosaccharides. These are complex carbohydrates bonded in such a way that human digestive enzymes cannot break them down for absorption by the body. These oligosaccharides are passed on to the large intestine, where a large bacterial population takes care of them in a fermentation process. The result is gas.

EMISSION CONTROLS

Any number of foods can produce that gassy feeling, but there are ways to lessen that effect in beans.

- Soak beans. Many of the troublesome oligosaccharides are leached out of the beans and into the water during the soaking process. The longer beans soak, the more oligosaccharides are drawn out. Throw out the soaking water and replace it with fresh water for cooking.

- Gradually add dried legumes to the diet. Start with the most easily digested ones—limas, lentils, and split peas— and eat a small amount each day or larger amounts twice a week. Work up to soybeans, considered the most difficult to digest.

- Eat more high-fiber foods. Those who seldom eat foods high in fiber have the most problems with beans.

- Cook beans thoroughly. Uncooked starch is a definite gas producer.

- Try Beano. This commercially produced supplement contains an enzyme that allegedly breaks down oligosaccharides before they are worked on by the gas-producing bacteria of the large intestine. It comes as a liquid, which is added to the first few bites of food, or as tablets, which are taken immediately before a high-fiber meal. Beano cannot be used during cooking, as its enzyme is inactivated at temperatures over 130°F.

Although studies on Beano are in progress, to date there has been only one study published. At the University of California at San Diego,

researchers fed 19 people a potent meatless chili: unsoaked navy, pinto, and kidney beans, cabbage, broccoli, cauliflower, and onions. With one meal, research participants consumed the chili mixture with Beano; with a second meal, they had a placebo. Less flatulence was reported with Beano, but not less bloating or discomfort.

Folkloric practices, passed from generation to generation or from friend to friend, carry the weight of experience rather than the proof of a laboratory, and experience with beans has supplied many solutions. The following is a list of anti-flatulence ingredients sworn as efficacious by bean-eating folks throughout the world.

- *Epazote*: In Mexico, everyone eats beans. So a handful of *epazote*, a weedy-looking herb, is thrown in the cooking pot with the beans for its flavor and reputed anti-flatulence properties.

- Ginger, turmeric, and asafetida: In India, these

seasonings are cooked with dried legumes as an aid in digestion.

- Kombu: Kombu is a sea vegetable in the large kelp family of seaweeds. It has traditional culinary uses in Japan, and it can be found dried in oriental and health food markets. To use kombu to reduce flatulence, simmer beans with a 1-in. by 3-in. piece, removing it when the beans are completely cooked.

- Fennel seeds: Chewing fennel seeds brings relief to some bean-eaters.

FARCE
This gas, or "wind," as it's been called for centuries in England, has inspired noted men of letters. Samuel Johnson, in his monumental *Dictionary of the English Language* (1755), gave a droll definition referring to a fart as "an ill wind behind." In contrast to this succinct witticism is Jonathan Swift's fanciful and inventive language contained in his 1722 treatise on the ill consequences of suppressing a fart, a pamphlet full of trenchant

wit and outrageous puns. He defines a fart as: "A Nitro-Aerial Vapour, exhal'd from an adjacent Pond of Stagnant Water of a Saline Nature, and rarify'd and sublim'd into the Nose of a Microcosmical Alembic, by the gentle heat of a STER-CORARIOUS Balneum, with a strong Empyreuma and forc'd thro' the Posterior by the Compressive Power of the expulsive Faculty." Swift also felt that "digestive wind" could easily be popularized "since the same authority that brought Hoop Petticoats into fashion can certainly bring farting into fashion. All it needs is some celebrated Toast of the Town to set an example."

Although strictures against "breaking wind" have long been a standby in dictums of polite behavior, there have always been adherents to the theory that restraining the natural emissions of gas can cause bodily harm. Benvenuto Cellini, in his 16th-century autobiography, relates that the Roman emperor Claudius planned an edict to legitimize the breaking of wind at the table after being touched by the sad tale of a man who was so modest that he "endangered his health by an attempt to restrain himself." Jonathan Swift floats a similar story about the unpopular King James I: "…for a gentleman dying while suppressing a fart in his presence, the King had immediately carved over the Gate, in capital letters, this inscription: HERE ALL FARTS ARE FREE."

In this country, our own man of letters, inventor and statesman Benjamin Franklin, applied his scientific mind to this subject. In a short essay, he enumerates the dire consequences of forcibly restraining "the Efforts of Nature to discharge…Wind": not only "great present Pain, but…future Diseases, such as habitual Cholics, Ruptures, Tympanies, &c., often destructive of the Constitution, & sometimes of Life itself." Taking to heart this problem of simultaneously maintaining one's health and social relations, this kite-flying *bon vivant* suggests a solution: "To discover some Drug wholesome and not disagreeable, to be mixed with our common Food, or Sauces, that shall render the Natural Discharges of Wind from our Bodies, not only inoffensive, but agreeable as Perfumes."

COOKING

The cooked dried beans of my childhood came in only one form—Boston baked beans. This traditional New England dish consists of beans soaked overnight and then baked slowly all day in a dark brown, glazed ceramic bean pot with salt pork or bacon, molasses, onions, mustard, and spices. (The proper ingredients can still provoke a heated discussion.) The result, always worth the wait, is a rich, mahogany-hued casserole with an aroma so tantalizing and evocative that it could pull in a missing family member from the far corners of the continent.

The popularity of dried beans has been hampered by the perception that all beans require this long, slow cooking. Most cooks today are interested in preparing healthful and delicious meals, but have limited time. Fortunately, there are options available that drastically cut cooking or preparation time for these high-protein, satisfying vegetables.

FACTORS THAT AFFECT COOKING

Although there are methods that can reduce the cooking time for dried beans, there are also inherent factors that will affect their preparation. For optimum cooking, it is also important to be aware of the following facts.

- Age: Dried legumes that have been stored longer than a year will require slightly longer soaking and cooking times. Soaking and cooking times increase with length of storage.

- pH: Cell walls of dried legumes are more soluble in alkaline conditions. This means they will take longer to cook in an acidic solution, such as one containing tomatoes, vinegar, or molasses. As a general rule, acidic ingredients should be added toward the end of cooking. Adding baking soda to the soaking water to create a more alkaline condition isn't a solution because it decreases the nutritional content of dried legumes. The more cell-wall material that is broken down, the more proteins and vitamins are leached out into the soaking water, which is then discarded.

- Salt: Beans will also take longer to cook in a salty solution. Sometimes, however, salt can be put to good use. For beans with fragile skins, such as large limas or soybeans, a teaspoon of salt added to the soaking water and then to the cooking liquid helps to keep the skins intact. As a general rule, salt should be added toward the end of cooking.

- Amount of water: The amount of nutrients in dried legumes can be affected by the amount of cooking liquid. Water-soluble vitamins and minerals, such as potassium and the B vitamins, leach out into the cooking liquid. To best retain them, use the smallest amount possible of cooking liquid so that little or no liquid remains when the legumes are done.

SORTING AND SOAKING

To ensure more uniform cooking and to eliminate water-soluble, gas-producing sugars, soaking is recommended for all dried legumes except lentils, split peas, and hulled and split *dals*. And before they are soaked or cooked, dried legumes should

be sorted through for pebbles and debris and then rinsed. If you've ever bitten down on a pebble in a cooked bean dish, you know how important this step is. Not all beans require this step; experience will reveal types and brands of beans that do not include foreign matter.

Sorting can easily be done by pouring the beans out into one layer on a rimmed baking sheet. After you pick out any foreign matter, transfer the beans to a container for storing. If you're cooking them immediately, place them in a colander and rinse them thoroughly.

Soaking, which causes dried legumes to absorb water and double or triple in size, is a simple step. There are several ways this can be done.

Quick soaking

This method takes about an hour. As a rule of thumb, for 1 cup of beans, use 4 cups of water. For each additional cup of beans, add 3 cups of water. Put the water and the sorted and rinsed beans in a large pot. Bring to a boil and cook for 2 minutes. Remove from the heat, cover, and let stand for 1 hour.

Beans should be soaked to reduce their cooking time and to leach out flatulence-producing carbohydrates.

Speed soaking

For a faster method, try speed soaking. It takes about 20 to 25 minutes and requires a pressure cooker. For 1 cup of beans, use 3 cups of water; for each additional cup of beans, use 2 cups of water. Put the water and the sorted and rinsed beans in the pressure cooker and lock the lid into place. (If using a jiggle-top cooker like the one in the photo on p. 58, use 1 tablespoon of oil for each cup of beans.) Bring to full pressure over high heat.

For small beans, such as navy beans or pigeon peas, remove the cooker from the heat and allow the pressure to fall naturally. After 10 minutes, release any remaining pressure with a quick-release method. (See p. 58 for information on release methods.)

For medium-size beans, such as pintos or kidneys, cook for 1 minute at high pressure. Remove from the heat and allow the pressure to fall naturally. After 10 to 15 minutes, release any remaining pressure with a quick-release method.

For large beans, such as chickpeas or runner beans, cook for 2 to 3 minutes at high pressure. Remove from the heat and allow the pressure to fall naturally. After 10 to 15 minutes, release any remaining pressure with a quick-release method.

Traditional soaking

Traditional soaking is usually thought of as an overnight process. In reality, it appears that there is little advantage in soaking beans for more than 4 hours. That means you can put the beans in to soak in the morning, and they'll be ready to cook in the afternoon.

For traditional soaking, use a large pot or bowl and 4 cups of water for the first cup of beans, with 3 cups of water for each additional cup of beans. Place the beans in the pot or bowl and add the water. Let the beans soak for at least 4 hours. If the beans will be soaking longer than 6 hours in a very warm room, place the bowl or pot in the refrigerator.

In all soaking methods, the soaking water should be thrown out. This is one step that can reduce the flatulence associated with beans.

PRESSURE COOKING

My pressure cooker has changed the way I cook beans. Inspired by *Great Vegetarian Cooking Under Pressure* by Lorna Sass, I now cook beans in minutes rather than in hours.

In the last decade, pressure cooking has been elevated to a new level with the introduction of newly designed models from Europe. Although their appearance is generally more streamlined than older models, the important difference is in the pressure regulator. Older-model pressure cookers—the type most of us are familiar with—have a separate, removable solid metal knob to fit over the vent for the purpose of regulating the pressure of the steam inside. A clamorous jiggling and hissing announces that full pressure has been reached. The pressure regulators on the newer designs are stationary or closely fitted, rather than loose and removable like the jiggle-top type, and are far more quiet. There is no clattering; at most, there may be a soft hissing.

If you use an older jiggle-top model for cooking beans, there are several steps that should be taken. If it's been a while since you've used the cooker, check the rubber gasket to make sure that it has not aged and dried out so much that it can't maintain a tight seal. You can check it by adding 2 cups of water to the cooker, locking the lid in position, and placing the cooker over high heat. If water drips down the outside

The new generation of pressure cookers (right) are safer and easier to use than the older, "jiggle-top" pressure cookers (left).

of the pot, or if full pressure is not achieved, replace the gasket. (Gaskets are available in well-stocked kitchenware or hardware stores or from the cooker's manufacturer.)

Cooking beans creates a layer of foam, which can result in bean matter clogging the pressure vent. In jiggle-top pressure cookers, 1 tablespoon of oil per cup of beans should be added to subdue this foam. You should also remain in the kitchen while the beans are cooking. If you hear a loud and disturbed sputtering, bring down the pressure immediately by placing the cooker under cold running water. When the pressure is com-

pletely down (check by gently lifting the pressure regulator), remove the lid. Clean the lid, vent, and gasket and remove any floating bean skins. Add another tablespoon of oil, replace the lid, and resume cooking.

Since the prime function of pressure cooking is to save time, whatever model you use should be brought up to full pressure as quickly as possible over high heat. When full pressure is reached, immediately lower the heat to maintain a steady high pressure. For most models, this means using the same amount of heat required for a simmer. Once a steady pressure is reached,

the cooking time begins. Manufacturers' instructions will give details on how to determine this steady high pressure. When pressure-cooking beans for a dish in which it is essential that they remain entirely whole and separate, such as a salad, it is a good idea to cook them for the minimal amount of time (see the chart on p. 61) and then, if necessary, finish them off by simmering.

When the beans have cooked for the recommended time, which is different for each type of bean (see the chart on p. 61), there are two methods of releasing the pressure.

For the *natural-release method,* turn off the flame or remove the cooker from the heat source and let it sit until the pressure has fallen. With beans, this takes 15 to 20 minutes. I prefer this method because the quick-release method sometimes causes bean skins to split.

In the *quick-release method,* pressure is released rapidly by running cool water over the cooker. Tilt the cooker slightly to direct water away from the pressure regulator.

With some newer models, the pressure can be released in a steady stream by manipulating a lever, a button, or the regulator itself.

As a general rule of thumb for cooking dried beans in a pressure cooker, never fill the cooker more than half full and do not cook more than the amount recommended by the manufacturer. The recommended amount for a 5¼-quart model is 2 cups of dried beans, and for a 7⅓-quart model, it is 3 cups.

TRADITIONAL SIMMERING

This familiar method may make up in comfort what it lacks in speed. Except for an occasional glance at the water level, you aren't required to pay much attention to the cooking beans. It's also a simple matter to check the beans for doneness. The most certain way to check is to remove a few from the pot with a slotted spoon, cool them under running water, and taste them. If there is any graininess or hardness, they need further cooking. Simmer for 10 more minutes and taste again.

To simmer soaked beans, place them in a pot and add water to cover them by 1 in. Bring to a boil, then lower the heat to a simmer. Skim off any foam and partially cover the pot. The beans should be covered by liquid throughout cooking.

USING CANNED BEANS

A stock of canned beans is a great convenience. Many types are available, particularly in ethnic sections of well-stocked grocery stores. Generally, pintos, chickpeas, black beans, and kidney beans are easy to find. Cranberry beans, favas, cannellini beans (white kidney beans), pigeon peas, and large limas are available, but they may take more effort to find.

Canned beans are usually quite salty. To cut down on sodium, drain and rinse them under cold water for 1 minute. Most recipes in this book start with cooked beans, but you can easily substitute canned beans.

SOME SPECIAL CASES

Their increasing popularity has made dried beans a current media favorite. It is easy to find information on them in newspapers, magazines,

books, television cooking shows, and the Internet. However, favas, soup peas, and shell beans remain relatively unknown and are often the subject of puzzlement.

Favas

Fava beans are often the source of culinary mystery and uncertainty. Although their pods are too fibrous to recommend them as a green bean, they are tender and delicious as a young shell bean. The younger they are, the more delicate their skin. Although the removal of their skin is based entirely on personal taste, there is a "thumbnail" rule that you can use as a guide: Generally, fresh favas under the size of a thumbnail have tender skin. At this stage, sautéed with a bit of finely minced onion and then cooked with fresh peas, they can form an exquisite rite of spring.

If the skins are substantial, their removal is a simple but labor-intensive process. Remove the beans from their pods and pour them into a pot of boiling water. After 30 seconds, drain them and put them in a bowl of cold water. Slit the skin of each bean with your thumbnail and pop out the bean. Once the beans are skinned, I like to simmer them with white wine or stock for 5 minutes, or until tender. A hint of sautéed minced garlic, shallots, or onions can be added, or, near the end of the cooking, add some chopped fresh herbs, such as mint, dill, or chervil. Finish this dish with a splash of fruity olive oil.

Dried favas are available in three different forms. The fastest cooking type are small hulled and split beans. These cook down rapidly and make a delicious soup base. *Ful medames*, the Egyptian fava, is a smallish bean with a relatively thin skin. These two characteristics mean that this type cooks in less time than the third type—the large favas, which appear to be the most commonly available. With their extraordinary size and rugged skin, large favas can seem a daunting project, but I find that they are excellent candidates for pressure cooking.

After large favas have been cooked, their skins can be removed by piercing them with the tip of a paring knife and slipping them off. I like to make a flavorful purée with these large beans, combining them with a bit of garlic and cumin seed

sautéed in olive oil, and then mixing them with a bit of lemon juice. They are also excellent in stews.

Soup peas

These traditional European dried peas are not readily available commercially, but the home gardener can easily grow them. Soup peas are very different from split peas. Dried split peas have their skin removed and are perfectly smooth little hemispheres of yellow or green. Soup peas are whole and are generally puckered and larger than split peas. Their colors are muted greens or light browns.

In cooking time and taste, soup peas are more like a bean than a pea. To prepare them, I soak them as if they were small beans, and then I simmer them for about 1½ hours with some chopped fresh parsley or summer savory. This legume forms its own rich brown gravy and is delicious over rice or a cooked grain. After soaking, soup peas can also be pressure-cooked for 3 to 4 minutes (with a natural pressure release) but will not produce a gravy with this method. However, by pouring off some of the cooking liquid

and simmering for 10 or 15 additional minutes, the remaining liquid will thicken.

Shell beans

These are the intermediate culinary stage of bean development, falling between snap and dry beans. The seeds are fully formed but have not begun to dry out, and their lumpy outlines are visible through their thinning pods.

Because of their higher moisture content, shell beans cook in much less time than dried beans. Their cooking time depends on their size— 15 minutes for small ones to 30 minutes for large ones. They can be counted on to keep their shape.

My favorite way to prepare shell beans is to sauté a bit of garlic and onion in olive oil until just beginning to turn golden. Add a bit of water, stir in the beans, cover, and braise until tender. Add salt, freshly ground pepper, and, if desired, a squeeze of lemon juice. Because they keep their shape so well, shell beans are wonderful in gratins and salads and combined with other vegetables. Like all beans, they take kindly to seasoning with most herbs and spices.

BEAN COOKING TIMES

Beans	Natural Pressure Release* (in min.) Soaked	Quick Release† (in min.) Soaked	Quick Release† (in min.) Unsoaked	Traditional Simmering (in min.)
Azuki	2-3	5-9	14-20	40-90
Anasazi & Jacob's Cattle	1-2	4-7	20-22	60
Black (turtle)	3-6	5-9	18-25	60-90
Black-eyed or Southern peas	—	—	10-11	45
Cannellini	5-8	9-12	22-25	90
Chickpeas	9-14	13-18	30-40	60-90
Cranberry (borlotti or Roman)	5-8	9-12	30-34	60
Fava‡	8-14	12-18	22-28	45-120
Flageolet	6-10	10-14	17-22	60
Great Northern	4-8	8-12	25-30	60-90
Lentils (brown)	—	—	8-10	35
Lentils (tiny black)	—	—	10-12	20-30
Lentils (red)	—	—	4-6	20-25
Lima (large)§	1-3	4-7	12-16	45-60
Lima (baby)	2-3	5-7	12-15	60
Mung	—	—	10-12	45-60
Navy (pea)	3-4	6-8	16-25	60-90
Peas (split, green, or yellow)	—	—	6-10	30
Peas (whole, soup)	4-6	8-10	16-18	60-90
Pigeon peas (gandules)	2-5	6-9	20-25	60
Pinto	1-3	4-6	22-25	60
Red kidney	5-8	10-12	20-25	60-90
Runner	8-10	12-14	17-20	90
Soy (beige)§	5-8	9-12	28-35	90-120
Soy (black)§	16-18	20-22	35-40	90-120

* To release pressure naturally, remove the pressure cooker from the heat source and let it sit until the pressure has fallen.

† To reduce pressure quickly, run cool water over the pressure cooker, tilting the cooker slightly to direct water away from the pressure regulator. Some newer pressure-cooker models have levers, buttons, or regulators that you can manipulate to release steam.

‡ For Egyptian ful medames, use the lesser amount of time.

§ Add 2 tablespoons of oil per cup of beans to subdue foaming during cooking. After soaking, remove any floating skins.

Copyright ©1994 by Lorna J. Sass. Reprinted by permission of William Morrow & Company, Inc.

RECIPES

APPETIZERS,
DIPS & SNACKS

Phyllo Triangles with
White Beans, Feta, and Dill
(recipe on page 66)

PHYLLO TRIANGLES WITH WHITE BEANS, FETA, AND DILL

For those who think beans are only heavy peasant fare, these light, lemony triangles prove otherwise. They make a great hot finger food for parties, and they can be frozen in bulk. If you have the freezer space, double or triple this recipe and freeze the triangles on baking sheets for future parties. When the triangles are thoroughly frozen, transfer them to airtight containers. Just before your guests arrive, transfer the frozen triangles to a buttered cookie sheet, brush with melted butter, and bake at 400°F for 20-25 minutes to a gorgeous golden brown. (Photo on page 64.)

1 package frozen phyllo sheets
1½ cups cooked white beans, drained well
1 cup crumbled feta cheese
1½ tablespoons lemon juice
3 heaping tablespoons chopped fresh dill
¼ teaspoon freshly ground black pepper
1 large clove garlic, crushed
½ cup melted butter or margarine

Thaw the phyllo sheets according to the package directions. Preheat the oven to 400°F. Grease a baking sheet.

In a large bowl, combine the beans, feta, lemon juice, dill, pepper, and garlic. (Use the filling immediately or it will become too watery.)

Take 3 sheets of phyllo dough and lay them out lengthwise. To keep the remaining phyllo sheets from drying out, cover them with a damp cloth. With a pastry brush, brush 1 phyllo sheet with melted butter, cover it with the second sheet, and then repeat the brushing and stacking to make a stack of 3 sheets. Cut the stacks in three 4-inch-wide strips (see the illustration below left). Be sure to work quickly so the edges don't dry out.

Place 1 heaping tablespoon of filling in the lower left corner of 1 strip. Fold the right corner of the dough over the filling to the left edge, forming a triangle (see the illustration below right). Continue folding the dough in this triangle pattern until you reach the end of the strip. Put filling on the other 2 strips and repeat the folding.

Place the triangles on the baking sheet. Remove 3 more sheets from their damp-cloth covering and repeat this entire process until all the phyllo is gone. (If you're freezing the triangles, cover them with plastic wrap and place them in the freezer.) Brush the tops of the triangles with the remaining butter and bake 12-17 minutes, or until golden brown. Let stand 15 minutes before serving so the filling cools a little.

Yields 12 triangles

Stack of 3 phyllo sheets, buttered and cut

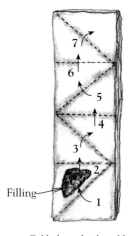

Filling

Fold along the dotted lines.

SPRING GREEN HUMMUS

*Lime juice, spinach, and a generous handful of parsley transform traditional
beige hummus into a spring-green delight. Make this dip a day ahead to let the flavors blend.
Serve it cold with crisp raw vegetables or warmed pita bread. (Photo on page 124.)*

1 cup dried chickpeas
   (2 cups cooked)
1 cup reserved bean stock
   or water
1 cup chopped raw spinach leaves
½ cup chopped fresh parsley
   plus extra for garnish
¼ cup tahini
2 cloves garlic, chopped
   or crushed
grated zest of ½ lime
1½ tablespoons lime juice
1 tablespoon olive oil plus extra
   for garnish
1 teaspoon salt
lime wedges, garnish

Sort through, rinse, soak, and
cook the beans by your preferred
method (see Chapter 7). Drain,
reserving about 1 cup of the stock.
If you're using canned chickpeas
or chickpeas that are not hot, simmer them in bean stock or water
until they're very hot. Drain,
reserving about 1 cup of the stock.

Put the spinach in a blender or
food processor, then add the hot
chickpeas (which will cook the

spinach slightly to bring out its
color and flavor). Process to a
smooth, bright green consistency.
Add the parsley, tahini, garlic,
lime zest, lime juice, oil, and salt.
Continue processing until the
mixture forms a thick paste. If the
mixture is too dry, add a little
reserved stock. Taste and adjust
the seasonings if necessary.
Garnish with the extra parsley,
lime wedges, and a splash of oil.

Serves 8

RUNNER BEANS
WITH CHIPOTLE AIOLI

The large size and mellow flavor of runner beans make them perfect
companions for a zesty sauce. I like them with Chipotle Aioli, an unexpected combination
of aioli, a garlicky mayonnaise, and smoky, hot chipotle chiles. In the past, homemade mayonnaise
had a well-deserved reputation for being difficult to make. However, a blender or food processor
has turned making this tricky emulsion into a simple undertaking.

1½ cups dried runner beans
  (3 cups cooked)
Chipotle Aioli, 1 recipe

Sort through, rinse, soak, and
cook the beans by your preferred
method (see Chapter 7). Drain.
  To serve, spoon the aioli into a
small bowl. Place the bowl on a
platter and arrange the beans on
the platter so they surround the
aioli, or simply place the beans in
a separate bowl. Place toothpicks
in the beans.

Serves 4-6

CHIPOTLE AIOLI
1 large egg
1 tablespoon red or
  white wine vinegar
three 1-inch canned chipotle
  chiles with adobo sauce
1 large clove garlic, minced
¼ teaspoon salt
¼ teaspoon sugar
1 cup vegetable oil

In a blender or food processor,
blend the egg, vinegar, chiles,
garlic, salt, sugar, and ¼ cup of the
oil at medium speed 30 seconds.
With the machine running, gradually add the remaining ¾ cup of
oil in a thin but steady stream.
Taste the aioli. If more chile taste
is needed, add some of the *adobo*
sauce from the can of chiles.

Runner Beans with
Chipotle Aioli (recipe this page)

TANGY BLACK BEAN DIP

This dip is a perfect match for thin, crisp corn chips.
The dip's tang comes from the cider vinegar. The vinegar also means that the
dip can be stored in the refrigerator for up to two weeks.

2 cups dried black beans
   (4 cups cooked)
1½ tablespoons vegetable oil
1 medium onion, chopped
1 medium bell pepper,
   any color, chopped
2 medium cloves garlic, minced
1½ tablespoons ground cumin
1½ tablespoons ground coriander
1 tablespoon chili powder
⅓-½ cup cider vinegar
salt, to taste

Sort through, rinse, soak, and cook the beans by your preferred method (see Chapter 7).

In a nonstick or heavy-bottomed frying pan, heat the oil over medium-high heat. When hot, add the onions, peppers, and garlic and sauté until the onions are translucent. Add the cumin, coriander, and chili powder and sauté 1 minute, stirring often. Add the vinegar and stir to dislodge any browned bits in the bottom of the pan.

In a food processor or food mill, purée the beans and the pepper mixture until smooth. Season with salt.

Yields 3½ cups

Note: If you're going to eat this dish within two hours of making it, use the lesser amount of vinegar. Use more if the dip will be served more than two hours later because it mellows with time.

SWEET POTATO BEAN CAKES
WITH TOMATILLO-LIME SALSA

*These sumptuous orange cakes topped with a tangy green salsa
make a hearty appetizer or main dish on a cold winter night. Use fresh tomatillos
if they're available. If not, canned tomatillos are a good substitute.*

1½ cups cooked sweet potatoes,
  mashed (about 2 medium
  sweet potatoes)
1 heaping tablespoon grated
  fresh ginger
1 large egg
⅓ cup chopped fresh parsley
1 tablespoon flour
pinch of ground red pepper
2 scallions, white and green
  parts, chopped
1 teaspoon ground allspice
½ teaspoon salt
1 tablespoon brown sugar
1 cup navy beans, cooked and
  drained well
¾-1 cup dry, unseasoned
  breadcrumbs
3 tablespoons vegetable oil
Tomatillo-Lime Salsa, 1 recipe

In a large bowl, combine the sweet
potatoes, ginger, egg, parsley, flour,
red pepper, scallions, allspice, salt,
brown sugar, and beans. Mix well
with a fork, taking care that the
beans don't become mashed.

Refrigerate at least 1 hour, or
until the mixture is firm enough
to form into balls. Roll the mixture into balls the size of golf
balls. Roll each ball in the bread
crumbs, then press the balls into
10 cakes with a fork.

In a medium-size frying pan,
heat 2 tablespoons of the oil over
medium heat. Add 5 of the cakes
and fry, turning once, until golden,
about 8-10 minutes. Remove
the cakes. Add the remaining
1 tablespoon of oil and fry the
remaining cakes. Serve with
Tomatillo-Lime Salsa.

*Serves 4-6 as an appetizer,
2-3 as a main dish*

TOMATILLO-LIME SALSA

2 tablespoons vegetable oil
1 small onion, chopped
1 clove garlic, minced
½ teaspoon or more chopped
  fresh jalapeño chile
1 teaspoon cumin
1 teaspoon coriander
20 tomatillos, or 1 can
  (28 ounces), drained well
¼ cup chopped cilantro
1 teaspoon sugar
1 tablespoon or more lime juice

In a large frying pan, heat the
oil over medium-low heat. When
hot, add the onions, garlic, chiles,
cumin, and coriander. Sauté until
the onions are translucent. Add
the tomatillos and continue
sautéing over low heat until the
tomatillos have broken down into
a sauce, about 5 minutes. Add the
cilantro, sugar, and lime juice and
continue cooking 1 minute. Serve
warm or at room temperature.

MOROCCAN SPICY BEAN PURÉE

*The addition of a group of lively seasonings transforms beans into a dramatic
dish in both color and taste. This purée has a spicy Moroccan flavor and the lovely warm
burnt-orange hue that I've seen in North African carpets. It makes a fine
spread on a pita and an enticing dip for raw vegetables or pitas.*

1½ cups dried cannellini or other
   white beans (3 cups cooked)
1 cup reserved bean stock
2 tablespoons olive oil
1 cup chopped onions
3 medium cloves garlic, minced
1½ teaspoons sweet paprika
¼ teaspoon ground red pepper
1 teaspoon ground cumin
juice of 1 lemon
½ teaspoon salt
¼ teaspoon freshly ground
   black pepper

Sort through, rinse, soak, and cook the beans by your preferred method (see Chapter 7). Drain, reserving 1 cup of the stock.

In a medium-size pot, heat the oil over medium heat. When hot, add the onions and garlic and sauté until the onions are translucent. Add the paprika, red pepper, and cumin. Sauté 2-3 minutes. Stir in the beans, stock, lemon juice, salt, and pepper and mix thoroughly.

Pour the mixture into a blender or food processor and purée until smooth. Taste and adjust the seasonings if necessary.

Serves 4-6

*top: Moroccan Spicy Bean Purée
(recipe this page);
bottom: Sweet-and-Sour Red Bean Salad
(recipe on page 83)*

TUSCAN PURÉED WHITE BEANS WITH ROASTED GARLIC

Because of the early and widespread popularity of the common bean in Tuscany (encouraged by the di Medicis, who probably saw an easy profit in it), the Tuscans have been called the mangafagioli, *or bean eaters, since the 16th century. This Tuscan-influenced recipe is very simple and very delicious. The roasted garlic adds a muted sweetness, but the amount used may vary, depending on its age, size, and variety. Add it gradually and taste as you go along.* ∽ *This purée makes a fine dip for fresh, crisp vegetables, but I think the best use is as a spread on thin toasted slices of a baguette topped with a slice of a summer-ripe tomato. Food of the gods.*

*1 cup dried white beans
   (2 cups cooked)
½ cup reserved bean stock
1 head of garlic
1-2 tablespoons fruity olive oil
salt, to taste
1 tablespoon chopped fresh
   basil, optional*

Sort through, rinse, soak, and cook the beans by your preferred method (see Chapter 7). Drain, reserving ½ cup of the stock.

Separate the garlic cloves, but do not peel them. Place them in a small, heavy-bottomed skillet, cover, and roast them over low heat 15-20 minutes, turning every 5 minutes. They're done when completely softened.

In a food processor, purée the beans, stock, oil, and salt. Clove by clove, squeeze the interior of the garlic into the purée and pulse between additions. Taste frequently and keep adding until the roasted garlic flavor speaks but doesn't shout. You can stop here or gild the lily by adding chopped fresh basil. Serve at room temperature.

Yields 2 cups

Note: I like to use a small covered cast-iron skillet for roasting garlic because it takes only 15-20 minutes rather than the 60 minutes required for roasting it in the oven.

GOLDEN NUGGETS

These delicate little snacks make fine hors d'oeuvres or picnic fare.
Bake them for an exceptional low-fat treat, or sauté them in a little oil for a
crisper coating. Lemon or lime wedges or a dip made of grated cucumber, yogurt,
and a bit of toasted cumin seed make a delicious finish for these snacks.

1 cup dried red lentils
2½ cups water
½ cup part-skim ricotta cheese
2 scallions, white and green parts,
   minced
1½ teaspoons fresh thyme,
   or ½ teaspoon dried
½ cup fresh breadcrumbs
salt and freshly ground black
   pepper, to taste
½ cup plain wheat germ
vegetable oil for frying

Rinse the lentils. In a medium-size pot, simmer the lentils in the water, partially covered, 20 minutes, or until they have cooked into a mush. Check the water level after 15 minutes to make sure there is enough. Drain.

If you're baking the nuggets, preheat the oven to 350°F. Grease a baking sheet.

Thoroughly mash the lentils. In a large bowl, combine the lentils, ricotta cheese, scallions, thyme, breadcrumbs, salt, and pepper. Use a tablespoon to scoop out the mixture and then roll it into little balls about 1 inch in diameter.

Pour the wheat germ into a shallow bowl and roll each nugget in it until completely covered.

If you're baking the nuggets, place them on the baking sheet and bake 20 minutes.

If you're frying the nuggets, heat a small amount of oil in a large frying pan over medium-high heat. Add the nuggets and fry, turning them until they are browned on all sides. Serve warm or at room temperature.

Yields 12-15 nuggets

Azuki Bean Dip

*Intriguing Chinese seasonings and the subtle sweetness of azuki beans make this
a perfect dip for sweet and mild-flavored vegetables, such as sugar snap peas, carrots, and celery.
Sichuan pepper provides a sweet and spicy flavor with an almost floral scent.*

1 cup dried azuki beans
½-1 cup reserved bean stock
1 heaping teaspoon Sichuan
   pepper, roasted and ground
1 scallion, white and green parts,
   coarsely chopped
4 teaspoons brown rice vinegar
   or rice wine vinegar
4 teaspoons soy sauce
1 teaspoon sesame oil
1 teaspoon grated fresh ginger
2 teaspoons minced cilantro
salt, to taste

Sort through, rinse, soak, and cook the beans by your preferred method until they're very soft (see Chapter 7). Drain, reserving 1 cup of the stock.

In a food processor, purée the beans, ½ cup of the stock, Sichuan pepper, scallions, vinegar, soy sauce, oil, ginger, and cilantro until completely smooth. Add more stock if the mixture is too firm. Season with salt. Serve chilled or at room temperature.

Yields 2 cups

Note: Sichuan pepper is reddish brown and looks like tiny, dried, unopened flowers. It can be found in Chinese markets or large supermarkets. To prepare the pepper, toast it in a small cast-iron skillet over medium heat 2-3 minutes, or until fragrant. Then grind it in a mortar and pestle or spice grinder. (I usually toast a couple of tablespoons and use what I need. I keep the remainder in a bottle with a tight stopper.)

*bottom: Azuki Bean Dip
(recipe this page);*
*top: Flageolets with a Mirepoix
(recipe on p. 140)*

APPETIZERS, DIPS & SNACKS

CHICKPEA MUNCHIES

*What food these morsels be. They vary from crunchy inside and out
to crunchy on the outside and soft on the inside. They're great for appetizers with drinks
and also make tasty, nutritious snacks. (Photo on page 129.)*

1 cup dried chickpeas
   (2½ cups cooked)
1 tablespoon olive oil
1 clove garlic, minced
2 teaspoons curry powder
½-¾ teaspoon salt
freshly ground black pepper,
   to taste

Sort through, rinse, soak, and cook the chickpeas by your preferred method (see Chapter 7). Drain and place on paper towels to dry.

Preheat the oven to 400°F. In a large frying pan, heat the oil over medium-low heat. When hot, add the garlic and curry powder. Sauté, stirring occasionally, until the garlic just begins to turn golden.

Add the chickpeas and stir to coat with the garlic and curry powder. Add the salt and pepper. Stir to combine and turn out the chickpeas into a large, shallow baking pan. Bake 25-35 minutes, or until crunchy. Serve warm.

Yields 2½ cups

Note: You can freeze cooked Chickpea Munchies and then reheat them at 400°F for 15-20 minutes.

BEANY POCKETS

*A platter full of these appealing little baked envelopes always tempts
friends and family to pick one up and try it. But one is never enough. Although best
served warm, the pockets are easily transportable, and they have proven to be popular picnic fare.
Beany Pockets are a small version of a popular local snack created by Barbara Tonne,
the owner of Global Naturelles, a small business that supplies Ithaca, N.Y.,
with tasty and nutritious portable lunches.*

¾ cup dried black or pinto beans
   (1½ cups cooked)
1 cup reserved bean stock
   or water
2 teaspoons vegetable oil
½ teaspoon ground cumin
½ teaspoon ground coriander
½ teaspoon chili powder
1 medium clove garlic, minced
½ cup chopped onions
¼-¾ teaspoon bottled hot sauce,
   optional
salt and freshly ground black
   pepper, to taste
ten 7-in. flour tortillas
1 cup grated cheddar
1 cup tomato salsa
½ cup minced scallions
½ cup grated carrots, optional

Sort through, rinse, soak, and cook the beans by your preferred method (see Chapter 7). Drain, reserving 1 cup of the stock.

Preheat the oven to 350°F. Mash the beans with a potato masher or fork, adding bean stock or water, if necessary, to achieve a soft not stiff consistency.

In a medium-size frying pan, heat the oil over medium-high heat. When hot, add the cumin, coriander, and chili powder and sauté 30 seconds. Add the garlic and onions and sauté until the onions are translucent. Stir this mixture into the mashed beans. Add the bottled hot sauce to taste, if desired. Season with salt and pepper.

Wrap the tortillas securely in aluminum foil and bake 10 minutes at 350°F. Remove and turn the oven up to 450°F.

To assemble, arrange bowls of beans, cheddar, salsa, scallions, and carrots, if desired, within easy reach. Place 1 heaping tablespoon of the beans in the center of a warmed tortilla. Layer on the other ingredients, ending with the cheese. Fold the left side of the tortilla, then the right side over the mound of filling. Then fold over each open end toward the middle, securely sealing the ingredients inside. Place the envelopes on a baking sheet with the folded sides down.

When all the pockets are assembled, bake 10 minutes at 450°F. Allow the pockets to cool slightly on the baking sheet and serve with the browned, folded side up.

Yields 10 pockets

SALADS

Greek Bean Salad
(recipe on page 82)

GREEK BEAN SALAD

*Purple-black kalamata olives, fresh oregano, the cool saltiness
of feta cheese, and summer-tender tomatoes and cucumbers make this hearty salad
both delicious and beautiful. (Photo on page 80.)*

1 cup dried cannellini or other
  large white beans (2½ cups
  cooked)
Greek Salad Dressing, 1 recipe
1 medium tomato, seeded and
  coarsely chopped
2 small pickling cucumbers,
  chopped, or 1 medium cucumber, seeded and chopped
¼ cup pitted and halved
  kalamata olives
¼ cup crumbled feta cheese
salt and freshly ground black
  pepper, to taste

Sort through, rinse, soak, and
cook the beans by your preferred
method (see Chapter 7). Drain.

While the beans are still warm,
pour them into a large serving
bowl. Add the dressing and mix
well. Cover and marinate at room
temperature at least 1 hour,
stirring occasionally to distribute
the dressing.

Shortly before serving, mix
in the tomatoes, cucumbers,
olives, and cheese. Season
with salt and pepper. Serve at
room temperature.

Serves 4

*Note: To remove a tomato's seeds, cut
the tomato in half horizontally.
Squeeze it to press the seeds out at the
same time you gouge the seed cavity
with the tip of a spoon. Most of the
seeds and surrounding gel should
come out.*

GREEK SALAD DRESSING
1 large clove garlic, minced
¼ cup fresh lemon juice
¼ cup olive oil
1 tablespoon fresh oregano,
  chopped, or ½ teaspoon dried

In a small bowl, whisk together
the garlic, lemon juice, oil,
and oregano.

SWEET-AND-SOUR RED BEAN SALAD

It's my love of bacon that keeps me from being a card-carrying vegetarian.
Although striving to lead a low-fat life, I give in to this indulgence on occasion and keep
a package of it in the freezer for the times when the desire for fat, salt, and sodium nitrite cannot
be denied. Although it's optional, bacon imparts a pleasant smokiness to this recipe.
This makes a great picnic dish. (Photo on page 73.)

2 cups dried small red chili beans
   (4 cups cooked)
Sweet-and-Sour Dressing, 1 recipe
1 cup sliced celery
½ cup chopped red onions
½ cup chopped parsley
4 slices cooked bacon,
   chopped, optional

Sort through, rinse, soak, and cook the beans by your preferred method (see Chapter 7). Drain.

While the beans are still warm, pour them into a large serving bowl. Add the dressing and mix thoroughly.

After the beans have cooled, add the celery, onions, parsley, and bacon, if using. Cover and marinate at room temperature at least 1 hour, stirring occasionally to distribute the dressing. Serve at room temperature.

Serves 6

Note: For this salad, I like the small red beans often used for chili. If they're not available, you can substitute red kidney beans.

SWEET-AND-SOUR DRESSING
½ cup red wine vinegar
½ cup vegetable oil
2 tablespoons sugar
1 teaspoon salt
½ teaspoon freshly ground
   black pepper
2 tablespoons warm bacon
   fat, optional

In a small bowl, whisk together the vinegar, oil, sugar, salt, pepper, and bacon fat, if using.

RED, BLACK,
AND WHITE SALAD

*Even when I fix this easy-to-make dish in the winter, it makes
me think of summer. There is something in the festive color combination
that brings back memories of picnics on a summer evening at Stewart Park, sitting
under voluminous weeping willows and gazing up the ultramarine length of
Cayuga Lake, one of the longest of New York's Finger Lakes.*

2 cups dried white beans
   (4 cups cooked)
1 large red bell pepper, chopped
½ cup Italian parsley, chopped
2-3 scallions, white and green
   parts, chopped
½ cup pitted and sliced
   kalamata olives
Fresh Basil Dressing, 1 recipe
salt and freshly ground black
   pepper, to taste

Sort through, rinse, soak, and
cook the beans by your preferred
method (see Chapter 7). Drain.

In a large bowl, combine the
beans with the peppers, parsley,
scallions, and olives. Add the
dressing and mix well. Season
with salt and pepper. Cover and
marinate at room temperature at
least 1 hour (4-5 hours is better),
stirring to distribute the dressing.
Before serving, taste and adjust the
seasonings if necessary.

Serves 8

FRESH BASIL DRESSING
⅓ cup fruity olive oil
3 tablespoons tarragon red
   wine vinegar
1 tablespoon lemon juice
1 tablespoon chopped fresh basil
1 medium clove garlic, minced

In a small bowl, whisk together
the oil, vinegar, lemon juice, basil,
and garlic.

BLACK BEAN,
BLACK BEAN SALAD

*This dish was really inspired by leftovers. If you've got an extra cup
of cooked black beans hanging around or some cooked rice, be sure to make
this salad of black beans and wild rice. Tossed in Chinese Black Bean Dressing, studded
with tangy dried cranberries, and garnished with a handful of toasted almonds, this is perfect
autumn fare. We eat it any time of the year, and come spring, a few
lightly steamed snow peas make this a beautiful picnic salad.*

*½ cup uncooked wild rice
    (1½ cups cooked)*
4 cups water
*1 cup uncooked brown rice
    (2½ cups cooked)*
*1 cup cooked black beans,
    drained*
*4 scallions, white and green
    parts, chopped*
1 cup dried cranberries
*1½ cups lightly steamed
    snow peas, optional*
*Chinese Black Bean Dressing,
    1 recipe*
*¾ cup slivered almonds,
    lightly toasted*

In a 2-quart saucepan, bring the
wild rice and 2 cups of the water
to a boil. Lower the heat and simmer, covered, 30-40 minutes, or
until the rice is fully cooked.

While the wild rice is simmering, in a 3-quart saucepan, bring
the brown rice and the remaining
2 cups of the water to a boil.
Lower the heat and simmer,
partially covered, 25-30 minutes,
or until the water is entirely
absorbed by the rice. Remove from
the heat, cover, and let steam
5 minutes.

In a large bowl, mix together
the wild rice and brown rice. Add
the beans, scallions, and cranberries. (If you're adding the snow
peas, do it now.) Add the dressing
and toss. Cover and marinate at
room temperature at least 1 hour,
stirring occasionally to distribute
the dressing. Mix in the toasted
almonds just before serving and
serve at room temperature.

Serves 8

CHINESE BLACK BEAN DRESSING

*3 tablespoons black bean
    paste with garlic*
*4½ tablespoons apple
    cider vinegar*
1½ tablespoons sesame oil
1 tablespoon grated fresh ginger

In a small bowl, whisk together
the bean paste, vinegar, oil,
and ginger.

*Note: You can find the black bean
paste in an Asian market or in the
Chinese food section of a well-stocked
grocery store.*

SOYBEANS
WITH SESAME SAUCE

The irresistible sesame-flavored sauce for this salad was inspired by some of the marvelous sauces for Chinese noodles. The sesame paste should be a Chinese sesame paste, not tahini, which lacks the rich taste of roasted sesame seeds.

1 cup dried soybeans
  (2½ cups cooked)
Sesame Sauce, 1 recipe
2 cups fresh bean sprouts
1 small cucumber, seeded and
  chopped into ½-inch chunks

Sort through, rinse, soak, and cook the beans by your preferred method (see Chapter 7). Skim with a slotted spoon to remove the bean skins as they rise. Drain.

In a large bowl, mix together the beans and Sesame Sauce. Cover and marinate at room temperature 1 hour, stirring occasionally to distribute the dressing.

Just before serving, add the bean sprouts and cucumbers, stirring thoroughly to combine. Serve at room temperature or chilled.

Serves 4-6

SESAME SAUCE
¼ cup Chinese sesame paste
  or peanut butter
¼ cup hot water
3 tablespoons soy sauce
1 teaspoon sugar
3 tablespoons red or white
  wine vinegar
pinch of ground red pepper

In a medium-size bowl, whisk together the sesame paste and water until they become a thin, smooth paste. Add the soy sauce, sugar, vinegar, and red pepper, stirring to combine.

Note: You may need to warm the jar of Chinese sesame paste in hot water and stir it with a fork to combine the oil and paste, if they have separated. If the sesame paste is not available, peanut butter can be substituted with good results.

*Soybeans with Sesame Sauce
(recipe this page)*

MINTED LENTIL SALAD

*I love this dish and could eat it for breakfast, lunch, and dinner. But
for those of you who can exercise restraint, it makes a fine accompaniment to chicken, grilled
vegetables, or a light soup. It's a refreshing and satisfying dish year-round.*

1 cup dried green or brown lentils

4 cups water

2 slices bacon

1 teaspoon minced fresh ginger

1 cup finely chopped onions

1 cup finely diced carrots

½ teaspoon ground cumin

½ teaspoon ground cinnamon

1 cup orange juice

salt and freshly ground black
  pepper, to taste

2 tablespoons red or white wine
  vinegar

½ cup chopped fresh spearmint
  plus extra for garnish

1 tablespoon olive oil, optional

Place the lentils in a saucepan and add the water. Bring to a boil. Lower the heat to simmer and cook the lentils until just tender, about 20 minutes. Drain and rinse with cold water.

In a heavy-bottomed frying pan, sauté the bacon until crisp. Remove the bacon and drain on a paper towel. Cut the bacon into small pieces.

Add the ginger, onions, carrots, cumin, and cinnamon to the frying pan and sauté 3 minutes, stirring occasionally. Add the lentils, bacon, and orange juice and simmer about 10 minutes, or until the liquid has been absorbed. Stir in the salt, pepper, vinegar, spearmint, and, if desired, 1 tablespoon olive oil to add some gloss.

Garnish with the extra spearmint and serve warm or at room temperature.

Serves 6

AZUKI SALAD WITH ASPARAGUS AND TOASTED WALNUTS

*Food, like smell, is a catalyst to memory. This salad will
always remind me of its genesis, a surprise visit from a long-absent friend
and lunch on a stone patio not far from the asparagus bed.*

1 cup dried azuki beans
   (2½ cups cooked)
¼ teaspoon salt
4 large asparagus spears, sliced
   into ¼-inch rounds
½ cup walnuts, coarsely chopped
1 scallion, white and green parts
½ cup sliced water chestnuts
Fresh Ginger Dressing, 1 recipe

Sort through, rinse, soak, and
cook the beans by your preferred
method (see Chapter 7). Drain,
place in a bowl, and add the salt.

Steam the asparagus 1-2 minutes, or until barely tender. Rinse
under cold water to prevent further cooking. In a toaster oven or
heavy-bottomed frying pan, toast
the walnuts until lightly browned,
then remove from the heat. With
a sharp knife, slit the scallion in
half vertically, then chop it into
thin horizontal slices.

In a large bowl, combine the
beans, asparagus, scallions, and
water chestnuts. Add the dressing
and toss. Mix in the walnuts and
serve immediately.

Serves 4-6

*Note: The toasted walnuts should be
added just before serving in order to
maintain their crispness. If this salad
sits for any length of time, it loses its
zing. If this happens, add a dash or
two of vinegar.*

FRESH GINGER DRESSING
¼ cup vegetable oil
¼ cup brown rice vinegar or
   rice wine vinegar
½ teaspoon grated fresh ginger
1 tablespoon soy sauce
½ teaspoon sugar

In a small bowl, whisk together
the oil, vinegar, ginger, soy sauce,
and sugar.

BLACK-EYED PEA AND TOMATO SALAD

Black-eyed peas originated in northern Africa and they have been a staple there for thousands of years. This unusual salad is adapted from Mediterranean Light by Martha Rose Shulman (Bantam, 1989). Its slight heat and Cumin Dressing make it a good choice for serving with grilled food. (Photo on page 102.)

1 cup dried black-eyed peas
  (3 cups cooked)
Cumin Dressing, 1 recipe
1 medium hot green chile pepper,
  seeded and minced
2 large tomatoes, diced
salt and freshly ground black
  pepper, to taste
¼ cup chopped cilantro or parsley

Sort through, rinse, soak, and cook the black-eyed peas until completely tender but not mushy by your preferred method (see Chapter 7). Drain well.

In a large bowl, mix the black-eyed peas, dressing, chiles, and tomatoes. (If the tomatoes are very juicy, add them just before serving so as not to dilute the dressing.) Season with salt and pepper. Cover and refrigerate 2-3 hours.

Just before serving, mix in the cilantro or parsley. Taste and adjust the seasonings if necessary.

Serves 6

CUMIN DRESSING
2 tablespoons lemon juice
2½ tablespoons balsamic
  vinegar
¾ teaspoon ground cumin
1 small clove garlic, minced
½ cup low-fat plain yogurt
1 tablespoon olive oil

In a small bowl, whisk together the lemon juice, vinegar, cumin, garlic, yogurt, and oil.

SOUTHWESTERN BLACK BEAN SALAD

A glorious salad for summer, when real tomatoes, as they're known around here, and fresh corn can be had. This dish has great visual appeal, with the deep black-brown of the beans mixed with the red, yellow, green, and white of the other ingredients, and a taste that lives up to its looks.

2 cups dried black beans
   (4 cups cooked)
1 canned chipotle chile
2 cups corn kernels, cooked
   briefly
1 large bell pepper, any color,
   chopped
1 large red onion, finely chopped
¼-½ cup finely chopped cilantro
Southwestern Dressing, 1 recipe
2 large tomatoes, coarsely
   chopped
salt, to taste

Sort through, rinse, soak, and cook the beans by your preferred method (see Chapter 7), adding the chile to the cooking water. Drain and discard the chile. If you're using canned beans, drain them and then add about 1-2 tablespoons of the *adobo* sauce from the can of chiles to give the beans some heat.

In a large bowl, combine the beans, corn, peppers, onions, and cilantro. Add the dressing and toss. Add the tomatoes and season with salt just before serving. Serve at room temperature.

Serves 8

Note: This salad can be refrigerated for a day and then brought out and allowed to reach room temperature. Just remember not to add the tomatoes until after you remove the salad from the refrigerator. Otherwise they'll become soggy.

SOUTHWESTERN DRESSING
1 teaspoon minced garlic
2 teaspoons ground cumin
1 teaspoon ground coriander
juice of 1 lime
2 tablespoons olive oil

In a small bowl, whisk together the garlic, cumin, coriander, lime juice, and oil.

CALYPSO SALAD

*Marinated in orange juice and infused with cinnamon
and allspice, this salad is a hot-weather treat. And best of all, most of it can be
prepared ahead of time so that come dinner all that's left to do is to sauté
the shrimp and chop a couple of mangoes and avocados.*

1¼ cups dried small red chili
  beans (2½ cups cooked)
2½ cups cooked brown or
  red rice
½ cup chopped red onions
2 tablespoons olive oil plus extra
  for frying
1 clove garlic, minced
2 tablespoons cilantro, finely
  chopped
Zesty Orange Dressing, 1 recipe
18 large shrimp, shelled and
  deveined
¼ teaspoon ground red pepper
½ teaspoon salt
1½ tablespoons lime juice
2 tablespoons chopped cilantro
2 mangoes, peeled and cubed
1 avocado, peeled and sliced

Sort through, rinse, soak, and
cook the beans by your preferred
method (see Chapter 7). Drain.

In a large bowl, combine
the beans, rice, onions, 2 tablespoons of the oil, garlic, cilantro,
and dressing.

In a medium-size frying pan,
heat the extra oil over medium
heat. Add the shrimp and red pepper and sauté until the shrimp are
pink. Remove from the heat and
add the salt, lime juice, and
cilantro. Combine with the bean
mixture. Just before serving, add
the mangoes and avocados.

*Serves 4 as a main dish,
6-8 as a side salad*

*Note: You can find red rice in
Asian markets.*

ZESTY ORANGE DRESSING
1½ cups orange juice,
  preferably fresh
1 tablespoon orange zest
1 teaspoon cinnamon, or
  1 cinnamon stick
1 teaspoon cumin seed
1 teaspoon whole coriander
1 tablespoon whole cloves
1 tablespoon whole allspice
1 teaspoon crushed red
  pepper flakes
1 tablespoon brown sugar

In a saucepan, combine the orange
juice, zest, cinnamon, cumin seed,
coriander, cloves, allspice, pepper
flakes, and brown sugar. Simmer
gently about 2 minutes. Remove
from the heat and cool. Strain
thoroughly and discard the cinnamon stick, if using, and the spices.

Calypso Salad (recipe this page)

CHICKPEA AND GREEN BEAN SALAD

*In the garden, green beans, like zucchini, can quickly go from
just enough to truckloads. This recipe is a refreshing way to take advantage
of the summer bounty of fresh green beans and cherry tomatoes.*

¾ cup dried chickpeas
  (1½ cups cooked)
2 cups fresh green beans, cut
  into ½-inch to 1-inch pieces
1 cup halved cherry tomatoes
¼ cup minced mild red or
  white onions
⅓ cup pitted and quartered
  kalamata olives
Thyme and Cumin Dressing,
  1 recipe

Sort through, rinse, soak, and
cook the chickpeas by your
preferred method (see Chapter
7). Drain.

Steam the green beans 3 minutes, or just until tender. In a
large bowl, combine the chickpeas, green beans, tomatoes,
onions, and olives. Add the dressing and mix well. Cover and marinate at room temperature at least
1 hour, stirring occasionally to
distribute the dressing. Serve at
room temperature.

Serves 4-6

THYME AND CUMIN DRESSING
½ cup plain yogurt
1 tablespoon olive oil
1 tablespoon lemon juice
1½ teaspoons fresh thyme, or
  ½ teaspoon dried
1 very small clove garlic, minced
¾ teaspoon ground cumin
½ teaspoon salt
¼ teaspoon freshly ground
  black pepper

In a small bowl, whisk together
the yogurt, oil, lemon juice,
thyme, garlic, cumin, salt,
and pepper.

SALADE NIÇOISE

*In this version of Salade Niçoise, a bed of marinated white beans
turns the traditional French dish into something a little more substantial. This beautiful
composed salad deserves the best ingredients you can find—sun-ripened tomatoes,
tender new potatoes, and imported European tuna.*

1 cup dried cannellini or
    Great Northern beans
    (2-2½ cups cooked)
Herbed Vinaigrette, 1 recipe
1 pound small red new potatoes
1 head of butter lettuce
2 cans (7 ounces each) solid white
    tuna, preferably imported
    European tuna
1 scallion, white and green
    parts, chopped
4 medium tomatoes, quartered
⅓ cup niçoise olives
2 tablespoons capers
3 hard-boiled eggs, halved
10 or more anchovy fillets,
    to taste
2 tablespoons fresh basil,
    finely chopped
freshly ground black pepper,
    to taste

Sort through, rinse, soak, and
cook the beans by your preferred
method (see Chapter 7). Drain.

Transfer the beans to a medium-
size bowl and drizzle with about
half the vinaigrette. Cover and
marinate at room temperature at
least 30 minutes, stirring occasionally to distribute the dressing.

Bring a pot of salted water to
a boil. Add the potatoes and
cook until just done. Remove from
the heat, drain immediately, and
slice the potatoes into rounds
¼ inch thick.

Line a large plate with the lettuce leaves and arrange the potato
slices around the outer edge of
the plate. Drizzle lightly with
3-4 tablespoons of the vinaigrette.

Spoon the beans into the center
of the plate and arrange chunks of
the tuna, scallions, tomatoes,
olives, capers, eggs, and anchovy
fillets in an attractive pattern on
top. Sprinkle with the basil.

Drizzle the remaining vinaigrette over the salad and give it a
once over with the pepper. Serve
at room temperature.

Serves 4-6

HERBED VINAIGRETTE
⅓ cup fruity olive oil
2 tablespoons red wine vinegar
1 tablespoon fresh lemon juice
1 tablespoon Dijon mustard
1 clove garlic, minced
1 tablespoon minced fresh basil
1 tablespoon minced fresh
    tarragon
1 tablespoon minced fresh
    oregano
1 teaspoon salt
¼ teaspoon freshly ground
    black pepper

In a small bowl, whisk together
the oil, vinegar, lemon juice, mustard, garlic, basil, tarragon,
oregano, salt, and pepper.

RED AND GREEN PASTA AND BEAN SALAD

The sturdy texture and nutty flavor of cranberry beans are great additions to this pasta salad. The vinaigrette uses less oil than most to bring out the bright, sharp flavors of the grilled red peppers and green olives. You can also add some chopped capocolla *or prosciutto and make a meal of it.*

1 cup dried cranberry, borlotti, or Roman beans (2 cups cooked)
1 jar (6 ounces) marinated artichoke hearts, drained
3 cups cooked al dente pasta, such as penne, small shells, or ziti
¼ cup chopped green olives
2 roasted red peppers, peeled, seeded, and coarsely chopped
Basil Vinaigrette, 1 recipe
2-3 cups chopped fresh spinach leaves
shaved Parmesan cheese

Sort through, rinse, soak, and cook the beans by your preferred method (see Chapter 7). Drain.

Chop the artichokes in half. In a large bowl, combine the beans, artichokes, pasta, olives, peppers, and vinaigrette. Just before serving, toss with the spinach and top with the Parmesan cheese.

Serves 4-6

BASIL VINAIGRETTE
⅓ cup fruity olive oil
¼ cup red wine vinegar
3 tablespoons chopped fresh basil, or 2 tablespoons prepared pesto
salt and freshly ground black pepper, to taste

In a small bowl, whisk together the oil, vinegar, basil, salt, and pepper.

LENTIL AND WHEAT BERRY SALAD

This cool and delicious salad is the perfect accompaniment to grilled meat or fish. It's simple to prepare, and you can add chopped tomatoes, scallions, cucumbers, peppers, and kalamata olives for a more bountiful version.

⅔ cup dried wheat berries
    (1 cup cooked)
3 cups water
¾ cup dried green or brown
    lentils (2 cups cooked)
Yogurt Dill Dressing, 1 recipe

Rinse the wheat berries and place them in a 2-quart pot with the water. Bring to a boil, lower the heat, and simmer, partially covered, 40 minutes, or until tender.

Sort through, rinse, and cook the lentils by your preferred method (see Chapter 7). Drain well.

In a large bowl, combine the wheat berries and lentils. Cool to room temperature. Stir in the dressing and serve at room temperature.

Serves 4-6 as a side salad

YOGURT DILL DRESSING
3 tablespoons fruity olive oil
1 tablespoon red wine vinegar
3 tablespoons chopped fresh dill
1 clove garlic, minced
1 tablespoon lemon juice
¼ teaspoon salt
½ teaspoon Dijon mustard
½ cup low-fat plain yogurt
freshly ground black pepper,
    to taste

In a small bowl, whisk together the oil, vinegar, dill, garlic, lemon juice, salt, mustard, yogurt, and pepper.

SOUPS

Indian Chilled Summer Soup
(recipe on page 100)

INDIAN CHILLED SUMMER SOUP

This exotic soup, adapted from one of Madhur Jaffrey's many fine recipes in
A Taste of India (Atheneum, 1988), makes an exciting addition to any summer-soup
repertoire. The preparation is unusual because the toor (or toovar) dal is cooked in a generous
amount of water, which it thickens. ∽ This process leaves you with about 3 extra cups of cooked
toor dal and a fine opportunity to create two soups from one—one for now, and one for the freezer.
The Toor Dal Soup with Vegetables (recipe on page 109) is a good way to take advantage
of the extra, thicker dal. (Photo on page 98.)

Soup:
2 cups nonoily toor dal
½ teaspoon ground turmeric
9½ cups water
¾ teaspoon whole cumin seeds
2 tablespoons lemon juice
1¼ teaspoons salt
½ teaspoon freshly ground
 black pepper
2 tablespoons chopped cilantro

Garnish:
2 scallions, white and green parts
2 small pickling cucumbers, or
 1 medium cucumber
1 large tomato
½ cup plain yogurt

For the soup: In a soup pot, simmer the *toor dal*, turmeric, and 9 cups of the water 1 hour, partially covered, or until the *toor dal* is quite mushy. Remove it from the heat and allow it to sit 5 minutes.

In a heavy-bottomed frying pan, roast the cumin seeds over medium heat until they begin to brown. Remove from the heat and grind in a mortar and pestle or spice grinder.

Using a 1-cup measure, ladle into a large bowl the thin liquid on top of the *toor dal* and enough of the thicker *toor dal* to make 5½ cups. Stir in the cumin seeds, lemon juice, salt, and pepper. Pour into a blender or food processor and purée until perfectly smooth. Taste and adjust seasonings if necessary. Don't be concerned if the mixture seems thin; it will thicken as it chills.

Pour the mixture into a large bowl. Add the remaining ½ cup water to the blender or food processor and pulse until all the *toor dal* mixture comes off the sides. Add the water to the soup. Cool until temperate and then chill for several hours in the refrigerator. Chill the serving bowls at the same time.

For the garnish: To prepare the garnish, slice the scallions into thin rounds. Drop them into ice water and refrigerate. If you're using pickling cucumbers, there is no need to peel and seed them. If using a larger cucumber, remove the skin and seeds. Chop into ¼-inch cubes. If the tomatoes are juicy, remove the seeds. Chop into ¼-inch cubes.

When you're ready to serve, remove the soup and the bowls from the refrigerator, giving the soup a few stirs. Remove the scallions from the ice water and drain on a paper towel. Add the cilantro to the soup and pour the soup into the chilled bowls. Garnish with the scallions, cucumbers, tomatoes, and a dollop of yogurt.

Serves 6

Note: Toor dal *is sometimes found in Indian markets with castor oil added as a preservative. For this recipe, use the nonoily type.*

Moroccan Bean and Bulgur Soup

If you have a cup of leftover cooked beans—any beans—this spicy and nourishing soup is a good way to use them. The cilantro mellows with cooking so that its assertive flavor is changed to a mild suggestion. The yogurt and lemon-wedge garnishes complete this soup, adding a cool and refreshing note.

1½ tablespoons olive oil
1 tablespoon sweet paprika
½ teaspoon turmeric
¼ teaspoon ground red pepper
8 cups stock
½ cup coarse bulgur
1 cup cooked beans
3 tablespoons chopped cilantro
salt and freshly ground black
   pepper, to taste
plain yogurt, garnish
lemon wedges, garnish

In a soup pot, heat the oil over medium-high heat. When hot, add the paprika, turmeric, and red pepper and sauté 1 minute. Add the stock, bulgur, beans, and cilantro and simmer, covered, 30 minutes. Season with salt and black pepper. Serve in bowls and garnish each serving with a dollop of yogurt and a lemon wedge.

Serves 4-6

BLACK BEAN SOUP
WITH LIME AND CUMIN

*My introduction to black bean soup was served
with a slice of lemon floating on its rich brown-black surface. Following
my host's lead, I sank the lemon with my spoon and smashed it against the bottom
of my bowl, releasing a snappy hit of lemon juice. My version of this smooth and elegant
soup uses a combination of lime (instead of lemon), cumin, and chipotle chile
for a piquant Mexican savor. It's a delight either hot or cold.*

*2 cups dried black beans
    (4 cups cooked)*
1½ tablespoons olive oil
1 tablespoon whole cumin
1 cup chopped onions
*4-5 cups reserved bean stock or
    bean stock and water*
½ canned chipotle chile
*¼ cup plus 2 tablespoons
    lime juice*
salt, to taste
lime slices, garnish
finely chopped cilantro, garnish

Sort through, rinse, soak, and cook the beans by your preferred method (see Chapter 7).

While the beans are cooking, heat the oil in a nonstick or heavy-bottomed frying pan over medium heat. When hot, add the cumin and brown it, taking care not to burn it. Add the onions and cook slowly until browned.

Drain the beans, reserving 5 cups of the stock. Purée the beans with 4 cups of the reserved stock in a blender or food processor. Add the onion mixture, chile, lime juice, and salt and process until velvety smooth. If the soup is too thick, thin it with the remaining 1 cup of stock.

Reheat the soup to serve it hot. To serve it cold, cool the soup to room temperature and chill it in the refrigerator 4-5 hours, or in the freezer, stirring occasionally, 1½ hours. Either hot or cold, garnish each serving of soup with a slice of lime floating in the middle and a sprinkling of the cilantro.

Serves 4

*top: Black-Eyed Pea and Tomato Salad
(recipe on page 90);
bottom: Black Bean Soup with Lime and Cumin
(recipe this page)*

SICILIAN
FAVA BEAN SOUP

*Fresh basil enhances the taste of this thick and flavorful
rustic Sicilian soup. The best bean for this soup is a small hulled-and-split fava
that cooks easily into a purée. The cooking time for whole favas is quite a bit longer, but you
can use them—just remove their skins after cooking. (Photo on page 153.)*

2 cups dried fava beans, hulled
   and split (4 cups cooked)
6 cups water plus extra if needed
2 tablespoons olive oil
1 cup chopped onions
1 cup chopped tomatoes, drained
¼ cup chopped fresh basil plus
   extra for garnish
salt and freshly ground black
   pepper, to taste

Sort through, rinse, soak, and cook the beans in the water by your preferred method (see Chapter 7).

While the beans are cooking, heat the oil in a soup pot over medium heat. When hot, add the onions and sauté until browned. Add the tomatoes and basil and cook over low heat 15 minutes.

When the beans have cooked into a succulent mush, stir in the tomato mixture and extra water, if needed, until the soup has the consistency of a thick pea soup. Season with salt and pepper.

Heat the soup 10 minutes, stirring frequently to prevent burning. Serve hot, garnished with the extra basil.

Serves 4-6

PUNJABI BEAN SOUP

*This dish is a good soup for a fall weekend. It's flavored by
a group of spices heated briefly in oil and then added to the soup. This group of spices
is called a baghar or tarka in India. I especially like biting down on the little bits of toasted
cumin seed found in this soup. Let the soup sit for 10 minutes after adding the baghar to let the
seasonings mellow. Mixing the yogurt with cornstarch stabilizes it and allows
you to reheat the soup without curdling the yogurt.*

1¼ cups dried red kidney beans
  (2½ cups cooked)
7 cups water
1 tablespoon chopped cilantro
1 medium onion, chopped
2 teaspoons grated fresh ginger
½ cup low-fat yogurt
2 teaspoons cornstarch
2 tablespoons lemon juice
1¼ teaspoons salt
1½ teaspoons garam masala
1½ tablespoons vegetable oil
1½ teaspoons cumin seeds
1 large clove garlic, minced
pinch of ground red pepper

Soak the beans overnight or speed-soak them (see Chapter 7). Drain the beans and put them in a large pot. Stir in the water, cilantro, onions, and 1 teaspoon of the ginger. Simmer 1 hour.

While the beans are simmering, mix the yogurt and cornstarch in a small bowl. Set aside.

When the beans are cooked, remove the pot from the heat. Remove 2½ cups of the beans and 1½ cups of the liquid from the pot and purée in a blender or food processor until smooth. Return this mixture to the pot and stir in the yogurt mixture, lemon juice, salt, and *garam masala*. Bring the soup to a simmer.

In a small pot or heavy frying pan, heat the oil over medium heat. When hot, add the cumin seeds and sauté 2 seconds. Add the remaining 1 teaspoon ginger, the garlic, and red pepper. Stir and sauté until the garlic is lightly browned. Add this mixture to the soup and stir to mix. Let sit 10 minutes before serving.

Serves 4

TURKISH LENTIL SOUP

*I love sweet-and-sour combinations. In this smooth soup,
I combined balsamic vinegar and dried apricots in a wonderfully
spiced base for an unusual and subtle piquancy.*

2 teaspoons olive oil
1 cup chopped onions
3 large cloves garlic, minced
1 large bay leaf
½ teaspoon cinnamon
¼ teaspoon ground cloves
½ teaspoon ground ginger
¾ teaspoon ground cumin
1¼ cups dried green lentils
8 cups water
2 teaspoons chopped cilantro
1 cup chopped dried apricots
1½ tablespoons balsamic vinegar
salt and freshly ground black
   pepper, to taste
paprika and finely chopped
   parsley, hot-soup garnish
dollop of plain yogurt,
   cold-soup garnish

In a soup pot, heat the oil over medium-high heat. When hot, add the onions and garlic and sauté until translucent. Add the bay leaf, cinnamon, cloves, ginger, and cumin and sauté about 2 minutes. Add the lentils, water, cilantro, and apricots and cook 1 hour, or until the lentils are completely soft.

Cool the soup slightly so it won't burn you, then add the vinegar. Remove the bay leaf and purée the soup in a blender or food processor. Season with salt and plenty of pepper. Reheat and serve hot, garnished with paprika and parsley. Or serve cold, with a dollop of yogurt.

Serves 4-6

*top: Turkish Lentil Soup
(recipe this page);
bottom: Lemony Lentils
(recipe on page 131)*

GRANDMOTHER SALVUCCI'S LENTIL SOUP

*Just a Taste wine and tapas bar in Ithaca, N.Y., is blessed
with the cooking of chef David Salvucci. Once, after a day of nasty winter adventures
in Boston, he returned home to find this comforting and delicious soup waiting
for him courtesy of his grandmother. He's never forgotten it.*

1 tablespoon olive oil
1 cup chopped onions
1 tablespoon minced garlic
2 cups green or brown lentils,
    rinsed
8 cups water or stock
1 cup diced potatoes
1 cup chopped tomatoes
1 tablespoon fresh thyme, or
    1 teaspoon dried
1 cup fresh spinach, roughly
    chopped
salt and freshly ground black
    pepper, to taste
shaved Parmesan cheese, garnish

In a soup pot, heat the oil over medium heat. When hot, add the onions and garlic and sauté until the onions are translucent. Stir in the lentils and the water and bring to a boil. Lower the heat and simmer gently 30 minutes.

Stir in the diced potatoes and simmer 10 minutes. Stir in the tomatoes and thyme and simmer 5 minutes. Stir in the spinach and simmer 1 minute. Season with salt and pepper. Serve topped with the Parmesan cheese.

Serves 6-8

TOOR DAL SOUP WITH VEGETABLES

This soup can be thought of as the cold-weather half of the
Indian Chilled Summer Soup (page 100). Whenever I make Indian Chilled Summer Soup,
there are 3 cups to 4 cups of leftover cooked dal *that can form the base for this wonderfully flavored,*
easy-to-prepare soup, which I freeze to use in the fall or winter. If you freeze this soup,
taste and adjust the seasonings after thawing and heating it.

2 cups nonoily toor dal
½ teaspoon ground turmeric
9 cups water
1 tablespoon vegetable oil
1¼ teaspoons ground coriander
½ teaspoon cinnamon
3 medium onions, chopped
3 cloves garlic, minced
2 cups stock
2 tablespoons cilantro, chopped
2 large tomatoes, chopped
1 large potato, peeled and diced
2 tablespoons lemon juice
salt and freshly ground black
    pepper, to taste

In a soup pot, simmer the *toor dal,* turmeric, and water 1 hour, partially covered, or until the *toor dal* is quite mushy. Remove it from the heat and allow it to sit 5 minutes.

In a large pot, heat the oil over medium heat. When hot, add the coriander and cinnamon and sauté 1 minute. Add the onions and garlic and sauté until the onions are translucent.

Add the stock, cilantro, tomatoes, and potatoes. Discard the thin liquid on top of the *toor dal* and add the remaining 3-4 cups of the thicker *toor dal* to the soup. Simmer over low heat 30-45 minutes, or until the potatoes are tender. Add the lemon juice and season with salt and pepper. Serve hot.

Serves 4-6

BLACK BEAN
AND TOMATO GAZPACHO

*This gazpacho is a perfect dish for a summer evening.
It's easy, refreshing, and beautiful. The soft succulence of the black
beans forms an intriguing counterpoint to the crisp, zesty flavor of tomato-based gazpacho.
This recipe is an adaptation of one by Jay Solomon, a teacher, chef, and cookbook author (his latest
is* Great Bowls of Fire, Prima, 1997) *who lives in Ithaca, N.Y.* ∾ *For a light supper,
serve this soup with cornbread baked with cubes of cheddar cheese and
chives and a fresh garden salad.*

¾ cup dried black beans
   (1½ cups cooked)
2 medium tomatoes, chopped
1 small mild red or white onion,
   chopped, or 4 scallions, white
   and green parts, chopped
1 green or red bell pepper,
   seeded and diced
1 cucumber, peeled, seeded,
   and diced
1 tablespoon minced cilantro
1 teaspoon hot pepper sauce
1 tablespoon red or white
   wine vinegar
¼ teaspoon salt
¼ teaspoon freshly ground
   black pepper
3 cups canned tomato juice,
   chilled

Sort through, rinse, soak, and cook the beans by your preferred method (see Chapter 7). Drain and cool.

Combine the tomatoes, onions, peppers, cucumbers, cilantro, hot pepper sauce, vinegar, salt, and pepper in a blender or food processor. Pulse 10-15 seconds, or until finely chopped. Transfer to a large bowl and stir in the beans and tomato juice. Chill at least 1 hour before serving. On a hot evening, I like to chill this gazpacho in the freezer 15 minutes before serving so that it is icy cold.

Serves 4-6

*Black Bean and Tomato Gazpacho
(recipe this page)*

West Indian
Split Yellow Pea Soup

*Warm in flavor and warm in color, this soup is a smooth
and rich terra-cotta hue. A rice salad and a loaf of cheese bread turn this soup
into a pleasing and simple supper. (Photo on page 147.)*

1 tablespoon vegetable oil
1 medium onion, chopped
½ teaspoon curry powder
½ teaspoon cinnamon
½ teaspoon dried thyme
1 bay leaf
½ teaspoon dried cumin
⅛ teaspoon ground cloves
1 cup split yellow peas
5 cups stock or water
2 cups tomato juice
salt and freshly ground black
   pepper, to taste

In a soup pot, heat the oil over medium-low heat. When hot, add the onions, curry powder, cinnamon, thyme, bay leaf, cumin, and cloves. Sauté until the onions are translucent. Add the peas, stock, and tomato juice. Bring to a boil, lower the heat, and simmer, covered, 1 hour, or until the peas are completely tender. Stir occasionally to prevent sticking.

When the peas are cooked, remove the bay leaf and purée the soup in a blender or food processor. Season with salt and pepper. Add hot water to thin, if necessary. Serve hot.

Serves 4-6

BEANS AND GREENS SOUP

*When the thermometer takes a serious dip as fall
and winter approach, this soup becomes the soup of the season.
You can use Swiss chard, kale, and fresh spinach in this soup. The choice
of beans is likewise at your discretion—limas, chickpeas,
or any in the common-bean clan are fine.*

1 tablespoon olive oil
2-inch piece of pepperoni,
    cut into ¼-inch cubes
1 medium-large onion, chopped
4 cloves garlic, minced
4 lightly packed cups chopped
    greens
1 stalk celery, chopped
1 medium carrot, chopped
1 tablespoon fresh basil, minced,
    plus extra for garnish, or
    1 teaspoon dried
6 cups stock or stock and
    tomato juice
1 cup chopped tomatoes, drained
1 cup cooked beans
½ cup uncooked rice
8-12 kalamata olives, sliced
salt and freshly ground black
    pepper, to taste
freshly grated Parmesan
    cheese, garnish

In a soup pot, heat the oil over low heat. When hot, add the pepperoni and sauté 3-4 minutes. Add the onions and garlic and sauté until the onions are translucent. Add the greens, celery, and carrots and sauté, stirring, until the greens have wilted.

Stir in the basil, stock, tomatoes, beans, rice, and olives. Bring to a boil, then lower the heat and simmer gently 45 minutes. Season with salt and pepper. Ladle into soup bowls and top with the Parmesan cheese and extra fresh basil.

Serves 4-6

AVGOLEMONO SOUP
WITH CHICKPEAS AND ASPARAGUS

A spring surfeit of asparagus was the inspiration for this soup.
The delicate crispness of lightly cooked asparagus provides a great textural foil
for the solid little globes of the chickpeas. The lemon silkiness of Greek avgolemono soup
enhances both textures, and its jonquil yellow gives it a spring color. It is
lovely for lunch or as a first course for an elegant dinner.

1½ tablespoons olive oil
1 cup finely chopped onions
2 medium cloves garlic, minced
6 cups stock
1 medium carrot, diced
1 cup cooked chickpeas
7-8 stalks fresh asparagus, sliced
    into thin rounds
3 large egg yolks
¼ cup lemon juice
salt and freshly ground black
    pepper, to taste
minced chives or dill, garnish

In a soup pot, heat the oil over medium heat. When hot, add the onions and garlic and sauté until the onions are translucent.

Add the stock and carrots. Bring to a boil, lower the heat, and simmer 10 minutes. Add the chickpeas and asparagus and simmer 5 minutes, or until the asparagus is barely tender.

While the asparagus and chickpeas are simmering, in a medium-size bowl, whisk together the egg yolks and lemon juice. Remove 1 cup of the simmering stock, let it cool 1-2 minutes, and then pour it slowly into the egg mixture, whisking constantly.

When the asparagus is cooked, remove the soup pot from the heat and stir in the egg mixture. Reheat gently over low heat, stirring constantly, until the soup thickens slightly. (Do not allow the soup to boil, or it will curdle.)

Season with salt and pepper. Serve at once garnished with minced chives or dill.

Serves 6

*Avgolemono Soup with
Chickpeas and Asparagus
(recipe this page)*

PURÉE OF FLAGEOLET SOUP

Flageolets are better known in France than in this country.
They have a distinct, delicate taste that defies close definition. But like
all beans, they readily absorb seasonings, turning this soup into a
smooth, creamy vegetable-and-herb-flavored dish.

1¼ cups dried flageolets
   (2½ cups cooked)
1½ tablespoons olive oil
1 heaping cup chopped onions
1 cup chopped carrots
1 clove garlic, minced
3 bay leaves
1 tablespoon fresh thyme, or
   1 teaspoon dried
6 cups stock
1½ cups milk
salt and freshly ground black
   pepper, to taste
chopped chives, garnish

Sort through, rinse, and soak the flageolets (see Chapter 7). Drain.

In a soup pot, heat the oil over medium heat. When hot, add the onions, carrots, garlic, and bay leaves. Sauté until the onions are translucent. Stir in the flageolets, thyme, and stock. Bring to a boil, lower the heat, and simmer gently 1-1½ hours, or until the flageolets are tender.

Remove from the heat. Remove the bay leaves and stir in the milk. Let the soup cool slightly and then purée it in a blender or food processor until creamy smooth. Reheat over low heat. Season with salt and pepper and garnish with the chives.

Serves 4

CARIBBEAN BEAN SOUP

*Inspired by seasonings and ingredients of the Caribbean,
this velvety soup is lovely served on a chilly night. It is a warm,
golden color, and its subtle coconut undertones may conjure up visions
of palm trees, turquoise water, and white sand beaches, especially
if you serve it with banana bread and fresh pineapple.*

1 cup dried white beans
   (2 cups cooked)
4 cups peeled and cubed
   pumpkin or winter squash
1½ tablespoons vegetable oil
1½ cups chopped onions
1 large clove garlic, minced
½ cup chopped celery
1 tablespoon minced or grated
   fresh ginger
½ teaspoon cinnamon
¼ teaspoon nutmeg
¼ teaspoon cardamom
3 cups reserved bean stock or
   bean stock and water
1½ cups coconut milk
1 cup orange juice
salt and freshly ground black
   pepper, to taste

Sort through, rinse, soak, and cook the beans by your preferred method (see Chapter 7).

While the beans are cooking, steam the pumpkin or squash until it is very tender.

While the squash is steaming, heat the oil in a soup pot over medium-high heat. When hot, add the onions, garlic, and celery and slowly cook until the onions are very tender and slightly browned. Stir in the ginger, cinnamon, nutmeg, and cardamom and cook 2 minutes.

Drain the beans, reserving 3 cups of stock. (Add water, if necessary, to make 3 cups of liquid.) Purée the beans, squash, onion mixture, reserved stock, coconut milk, and orange juice in a blender or food processor. Return the soup to the pot and season with salt and pepper. Reheat and serve.

Serves 4-6

POTAGE
À LA BRETONNE

This delicious and comforting soup is adapted from
New Recipes from Moosewood Restaurant (*Ten Speed Press, 1987*)
and has been one of my favorites since my days as a cook there.

1¼ cups dried navy beans
    (3 cups cooked)
7 cups stock or water
2 tablespoons butter
3 leeks, white part only,
    sliced thin
2 cups chopped onions
2 cloves garlic, minced
2 bay leaves
1½ teaspoons dried tarragon
3 medium tomatoes, chopped
¼ cup fresh lemon juice
1 cup light cream or half-and-half
salt and freshly ground black
    pepper, to taste

Sort through, rinse, soak, and cook the beans in the stock by your preferred method (see Chapter 7). Reserve the bean stock.

In a soup pot, melt the butter over medium-low heat. Add the leeks, onions, and garlic and sauté until the onions are translucent. Add the bay leaves and tarragon and sauté until the onions begin to brown. Add the tomatoes and simmer 10 minutes. Add the beans and reserved stock and simmer gently 10-15 minutes, stirring occasionally to prevent sticking.

Remove the bay leaves and purée the soup in a blender or food processor. Stir in the lemon juice and the cream. Reheat without boiling. Season with salt and pepper and serve hot.

Serves 6

MISO SOUP
WITH AZUKI BEANS

This is a richly flavored, dense soup—a meal in a bowl.
A flavorful azuki bean base is combined with thinly sliced vegetables, tofu,
and rice. You can also add extra vegetables, such as slivered fresh spinach, snow peas,
or julienned daikon. Serve with a light cucumber salad for a real palate pleaser.

1 cup dried azuki beans
   (2 cups cooked)
2 pieces (about 6 inches long)
   kombu
8 cups water
½ cup red miso
1 tablespoon bonito flakes,
   optional
2 carrots, sliced thin on
   the diagonal
2 celery stalks, sliced thin on
   the diagonal
1 cup cooked white or brown rice
1 cake soft tofu, cubed
soy sauce, to taste
4 scallions, white and green parts,
   sliced thin, garnish

Sort through, rinse, soak, and cook the beans until quite mushy by your preferred method (see Chapter 7). Purée in a food processor with a bit of their cooking stock. Set aside.

Combine the kombu and water in a large soup pot and simmer over low heat 20 minutes. Remove the kombu and discard it. Add the beans, miso, bonito, carrots, and celery and continue cooking on low heat (taking care not to boil the soup) until the vegetables are tender.

Add the rice and tofu. Check the soup for saltiness, then add the soy sauce to taste. Heat through. Top with sliced scallions just before serving.

Serves 4-6

Note: Kombu, a member of the kelp family of seaweeds, adds flavor, and many people find that it makes beans easier to digest. It can be found in Asian and whole-food markets.

SIDE DISHES

Curried Black-Eyed Peas
(recipe on page 122)

CURRIED BLACK-EYED PEAS

In this country, we associate black-eyed peas with the South. However,
they originated in West Africa (where they remain an important staple) and were found
in India thousands of years before they made their appearance on this continent. This dish
makes a fine accompaniment for any simple, straightforward entrée, or try it with basmati rice,
mango chutney, and a plate of sliced fresh fruit. (Photo on page 120.)

1 cup dried black-eyed peas
  (2 cups cooked)
1 tablespoon vegetable oil
1 teaspoon whole cumin seeds
1 medium onion, sliced thin
3 medium onions, minced
1 large clove garlic, minced
1 teaspoon sugar
1 teaspoon turmeric
⅛-¼ teaspoon ground red pepper
2 teaspoons ground coriander
2 medium tomatoes, chopped
1 teaspoon garam masala
1 teaspoon grated fresh ginger
2 teaspoons lemon juice
salt, to taste
fresh mint, chopped, garnish
grated coconut, garnish

Sort through, rinse, soak, and cook the black-eyed peas by your preferred method (see Chapter 7).

In a 3-quart saucepan, heat the oil over medium-high heat. When hot, add the cumin seeds and toast them 2 minutes until darkened but not burnt. (There will also be a change in aroma that lets you know when the right stage has been reached.) Add the sliced onions and sauté until translucent. Add the minced onions and garlic and cook until slightly browned.

Mix in the sugar, turmeric, red pepper, coriander, and tomatoes. Stir well, cover, and simmer 10 minutes, or until the tomatoes are mushy.

Add the black-eyed peas, stir, and simmer 5-10 minutes more. Remove from the heat. Add the *garam masala*, ginger, and lemon juice. Season with salt. Garnish with the mint and coconut. Serve hot.

Serves 6

BIG A'S BIG BEAN CAKE

This bean cake has a thin, crisp crust and a surprisingly light, delicate texture. For a quick dish, serve it topped with your favorite canned salsa and low-fat sour cream. For something special, try it with some homemade Salsa Fresca (recipe follows). You can serve this bean cake as an entrée with warmed tortillas and a crisp green salad of orange sections and thin slices of mild onion, or you can cut it into wedges and serve it as a companion to light chicken, fish, or vegetarian main dishes.

1 tablespoon vegetable oil
1 medium onion, chopped
2 medium cloves garlic, minced
1 small poblano, Hungarian wax,
   or other moderately hot chile,
   seeded and chopped
1 teaspoon ground cumin
½ teaspoon ground coriander
2 eggs
¼-½ teaspoon salt
2 cups cooked and drained pinto,
   black, or anasazi beans
low-fat sour cream
Salsa Fresca, 1 recipe
chopped cilantro, garnish

In a medium-size frying pan, heat the oil over medium heat. When hot, add the onions, garlic, and chiles and sauté until the onions are translucent. Add the cumin and coriander and sauté briefly until aromatic.

In a food processor, pulse the eggs and salt briefly to blend. Add the beans and purée. Add the chile mixture and pulse briefly just to mix.

Grease an 8-inch nonstick frying pan. Transfer the bean mixture to the frying pan. Smooth the surface and cook, uncovered, over low heat 10 minutes. Cover and cook 5 minutes more. Loosen the edges with a spatula. Flip the bean cake from the pan to a serving plate. Spoon first the sour cream over the top and then the Salsa Fresca. Garnish with the cilantro and serve hot.

Serves 4 as a side dish,
2 as an entrée

Note: To ensure the bean cake's easy removal, I recommend a nonstick frying pan.

SALSA FRESCA

3 large ripe tomatoes, chopped
1 small mild onion, minced
2 medium cloves garlic, minced
1-2 jalapeño chiles, seeded and
   minced (for a milder salsa, use
   Anaheim chiles)
2 tablespoons chopped cilantro
2 tablespoons lemon juice, lime
   juice, or vinegar
salt and freshly ground black
   pepper, to taste

In a medium-size bowl, combine the tomatoes, onions, garlic, chiles, cilantro, lemon juice, salt, and pepper. Cover and let sit at room temperature 1 hour to marry flavors. This salsa is best fresh, but any leftovers can be simmered briefly and then kept refrigerated for up to a week.

Yields 3 cups

LIMA BEANS IN ANCHO CHILE AND BLACK OLIVE SAUCE

*This dish of Peruvian origin is guaranteed to set taste buds aquiver
with its savory combination of kalamata olives and ancho chiles. The garnish is important
for texture and color—the crunch and tang of the celery and scallions provide
a counterpoint to the soft succulence of the limas.*

2 cups dried large lima beans
   (4 cups cooked)
1 dried ancho chile
½ cup very hot water
½ canned chipotle chile
1 teaspoon chopped fresh ginger
1 cup pitted kalamata olives
1½ tablespoons olive oil
2 medium cloves garlic, minced
salt and freshly ground black
   pepper, to taste
sliced scallions, white and green
   parts, garnish
minced celery, garnish

Sort through, rinse, soak, and cook the beans by your preferred method (see Chapter 7).

While the beans are cooking, break the ancho chile into small pieces and place them in a small bowl with the water. Add the chipotle chile and ginger to the water and soak 15 minutes. Pour the mixture into a blender, add the olives, and process at high speed until smooth.

In a heavy-bottomed pan, heat the oil over low heat. When hot, add the garlic and sauté until it starts to turn golden. Add the olive mixture and sauté 5 minutes. Drain the beans and add them. Cook 10 minutes, stirring occasionally to prevent sticking.

Season with salt and pepper. Serve the beans hot, garnished with a generous amount of scallions and celery sprinkled over the top.

Serves 4-6

*bottom: Lima Beans in Ancho Chile and Black
Olive Sauce (recipe this page);
top: Spring Green Hummus (recipe on page 67)*

CRANBERRY BEANS
WITH ARUGULA

*As the coolness of spring is slowly replaced by the heat of summer, the arugula in
my garden also takes on a seasonal heat as it goes to seed. This dish is a fine use for this green as
it becomes a little too mature and strong-tasting for fresh salads. Cooking tones down the intensity
and transforms the arugula into a piquant seasoning. If you're using young arugula, you may need to
increase the amount. This is a superb accompaniment to polenta and vegetables.*

1½ cups dried cranberry beans,
  borlotti, or Roman beans
  (3 cups cooked)
2 tablespoons olive oil plus extra
  for serving
½ cup chopped arugula
½ teaspoon salt
¼ teaspoon freshly ground
  black pepper

Sort through, rinse, soak, and
cook the beans by your preferred
method (see Chapter 7). Drain.

In a small pan, heat the oil over
low heat. When hot, add the
arugula and sauté just until
wilted. Remove from the heat
and mix with the beans. Add the
salt and pepper and a splash of
oil. Serve warm.

Serves 4-6

GALLO PINTO
AND FRIED PLANTAINS

As anyone who has traveled in Costa Rica can tell you, Gallo Pinto is the national dish. Its name translates to "Speckled Hen," and you can get it at most restaurants morning, noon, and night. It's usually served with bottled hot sauce or Salsa Lizano, a commercial product that tastes sort of like a creamy Worcestershire sauce. Leftover Gallo Pinto makes a great breakfast with scrambled eggs. For supper, it is delicious with a cheese omelet and a green salad. Gallo Pinto is also delicious with fried plantains and is often served with them on the side (recipe follows).

1½ cups dried black beans
   (3 cups cooked)
¼ cup reserved bean stock
2 tablespoons vegetable oil
2 medium onions, chopped
1 red or green bell pepper,
   chopped
3 cloves garlic, minced
2 cups cooked rice
1¼ teaspoons salt
freshly ground black pepper,
   to taste
bottled hot sauce

Sort through, rinse, soak, and cook the beans by your preferred method (see Chapter 7). Drain, reserving ¼ cup of the stock.

In a large frying pan, heat the oil over low heat. When hot, add the onions, peppers, and garlic and sauté 5-10 minutes just until the onions begin to brown. Add the rice, beans, stock, salt, and pepper. Cook, stirring frequently, until all the stock is absorbed. Serve hot, accompanied by a bottle of hot sauce.

Serves 6-8

FRIED PLANTAINS
2 yellow or brown plantains
3 tablespoons vegetable oil
salt, to taste

Peel the plantains as you would bananas and cut each one horizontally into 3 equal sections. Cut each section vertically into ¼-inch slices.

Heat the oil in a large frying pan over medium heat. Fry the plantain slices on each side until browned, about 2-3 minutes per side. Drain on paper towels, sprinkle with salt, and serve hot.

Serves 4

Note: Plantains, a large variety of banana, can be found either green, half-ripe with yellow skins, or fully ripe with very dark, almost black skins. Either the half-ripe or fully ripe ones will do for this recipe.

KOREAN SOYBEANS

*Although soybeans are known for their versatility, it wasn't until I tried this dish
that I knew how tasty they could be. Simmering them in a soy-sauce base until they absorb
the flavor imparts a brown glaze and a wonderfully rich taste to the beans.*

1 cup dried soybeans
  (2 cups cooked)
¼ cup reduced-sodium soy sauce
¾ cup water
1 tablespoon sugar
1 teaspoon sesame oil
1 tablespoon sesame seeds

Sort through, rinse, soak, and cook the beans by your preferred method (see Chapter 7). Skim the cooking water with a slotted spoon to remove the bean skins. Drain.

In a medium-size pot, combine the soy sauce, water, and sugar. Add the soybeans. Bring to a boil. Lower the heat and simmer, partially covered, about 25-30 min-utes, or until all the liquid has been absorbed. Remove from the heat and stir in the sesame oil.

In a toaster oven or heavy frying pan, toast the sesame seeds until lightly browned. Sprinkle on top of the beans. Serve hot.

Serves 4

*top: Baked Cannellini Beans
with Lemon and Rosemary (recipe on page 138);
center: Korean Soybeans (recipe this page);
bottom: Chickpea Munchies (recipe on page 78)*

Cannellini Beans with Greens

Years ago, a friend who is a wonderful cook demonstrated
for me what has become my favorite method of cooking kale and Swiss chard.
He sautéed the greens in olive oil with lots of garlic and added a chopped tomato after
the greens had wilted. Added to succulent white beans, the greens' sharpness and
full flavor make this a deeply satisfying dish.

1½ cups dried cannellini beans
(3 cups cooked)
3 tablespoons olive oil
4 medium cloves garlic, minced
5 cups chopped kale or
Swiss chard
3 tablespoons water
1 large tomato, chopped
salt and freshly ground black
pepper, to taste
grated Parmesan or Romano
cheese

Sort through, rinse, soak, and cook the beans by your preferred method (see Chapter 7). Drain.

In a frying pan, heat the oil over low heat. When hot, add the garlic and sauté until it just begins to turn golden. Add the greens and toss to coat with the oil and garlic. Add the water, cover, and steam 4-5 minutes, or until the greens have wilted. Add the tomatoes and cook over low heat 10-15 minutes, or until the greens are completely tender and the liquid has mostly been absorbed.

In a large bowl, mix the beans and greens. Season with salt and a generous amount of pepper. Top with Parmesan or Romano cheese.

Serves 4-6

LEMONY LENTILS

Lemons can perk up many grain, bean, and vegetable dishes.
Here the combination of lemon, cinnamon, fresh ginger, sautéed onions, and garlic
lifts lentils out of the ordinary and turns them into a dish of distinction.

2½ tablespoons vegetable oil
2 medium onions, sliced thin
two 2-inch pieces of cinnamon
   stick
1½ teaspoons grated fresh ginger
⅛ teaspoon ground red pepper
2 cups dried green lentils,
   sorted through and rinsed
2½ cups stock or water
3 bay leaves
1 lemon, rinsed well
1 medium onion, chopped
1 clove garlic, minced
salt and freshly ground black
   pepper, to taste
finely chopped cilantro, garnish
lemon wedges, garnish

In a large saucepan, heat 1½ tablespoons of the oil over medium-low heat. Add the sliced onions and sauté until translucent. Add the cinnamon stick pieces, ginger, and red pepper and sauté, stirring occasionally, until the onions begin to brown.

Stir in the lentils and add the stock. Bring to a boil and lower the heat to simmer. Add the bay leaves. Cut the lemon in half, discard the seeds, and squeeze the juice into the lentils. Cut each squeezed lemon half in half again and stir them into the lentils.

Simmer, covered, 45-50 minutes, or until the lentils are tender. Check during the last part of the cooking to make sure there is enough water, and add more if necessary. Remove the cinnamon pieces, bay leaves, and lemon shells.

In a small pan, heat the remaining 1 tablespoon of oil over medium-low heat. When hot, add the chopped onions and garlic and sauté until the onions are browned. Stir into the lentils. Season with salt and black pepper. Serve hot, garnished with the cilantro and lemon wedges.

Serves 4-6

MOONG DAL WITH SPINACH AND TOMATOES

While many cooked dals end up like heavy, thick soups,
this recipe produces a remarkably fresh-tasting bean and vegetable melange.
The moong dal is cooked until tender, but it retains its shape.

¾ cup split unhulled moong dal
1½ cups water
4 packed cups fresh spinach
3 medium tomatoes, chopped
1 medium mild onion, chopped
pinch of ground red pepper
salt, to taste
¼-⅓ cup plain yogurt

In a medium-size pot, combine the *moong dal* and water and simmer 25-30 minutes. Check frequently to make sure there is enough water, and add more if necessary.

While the *moong dal* is cooking, steam the spinach just until wilted. Turn it onto a cutting board and chop.

Drain the *moong dal* and return it to the pot. Add the spinach, tomatoes, onions, and red pepper. Season with salt. Cook 5 minutes, remove from the heat, and stir in the yogurt. Serve warm.

Serves 4

Note: Moong dal *is split mung beans and can be found either hulled or unhulled. In this recipe, unhulled* moong dal *produces the best texture.*

top: Moong Dal *with Spinach and Tomatoes*
(recipe this page);
bottom: Pigeon Peas *with Sofrito and Saffron*
Rice *(recipe on page 161)*

PURÉE OF
CURRIED GREEN PEAS

*This dish is luscious in taste, texture, and color. The spices meld with the
peas into a velvety-soft green purée, which goes beautifully with a vegetable gratin and
cornbread or with a ham, sausage, or chicken entrée. You'll need a food processor for
this purée, which is just thick enough to bring a blender to its knees.*

1 tablespoon olive oil
1 medium onion, chopped
1 medium clove garlic, minced
½ teaspoon curry powder
¼ teaspoon cinnamon
⅛ teaspoon ground cloves
⅛ teaspoon ground red pepper
2 cups dried green split peas
4 cups water
salt and freshly ground black
   pepper, to taste
chopped mint, garnish
chopped hard-boiled egg, garnish

In a 3-quart saucepan, heat the oil over medium-high heat. When hot, add the onions and garlic and sauté until the onions are translucent. Add the curry powder, cinnamon, cloves, and red pepper and sauté 1 minute.

Add the peas and water and bring to a boil. Lower the heat and simmer, covered, 1 hour, checking occasionally to make sure there is sufficient liquid.

When the peas are completely tender, season with salt and pepper. Remove from the heat. Purée in a food processor until smooth. Garnish with the mint and eggs and serve hot.

Serves 4-6

Note: When it's cold, this dish turns into a substance that could be used as a medium for sculpture. To reheat it without a microwave, break it up and add it to a small amount of boiling water in a pan. Lower the heat and stir frequently until warmed, adding more water if necessary.

MASOOR DAL WITH OKRA

*Masoor dal, also known as red lentils, is the bright salmon-orange
interior of a particular type of lentil that has had its hull removed. When it is cooked,
this identifying color is changed to a light tan. Because masoor dal has no hulls, it cooks quickly.
Although dals are generally served as a side dish in an Indian meal, there is no reason why they need to be
so restricted. This dish, for example, would be delicious with grilled or roasted chicken. It is
also a fine use of okra, which is not cooked long enough to lose its texture.
For the best results, use young okra, 3-4 inches long.*

2 tablespoons vegetable oil
1 tablespoon cumin seeds
2 cinnamon sticks, broken in half
2 medium onions, sliced
½ teaspoon turmeric
1-2 hot chiles, such as jalapeño
    or serrano, seeded and minced
3 tablespoons minced cilantro
2 cups masoor dal, sorted
    through and rinsed
1 large tomato, chopped
1½ tablespoons tomato paste
20 to 25 okra, sliced into 1-inch
    sections, or 1 package
    (10 ounces) frozen okra
5 cups water
1 teaspoon lemon juice
salt and freshly ground black
    pepper, to taste
1 teaspoon garam masala

In a large pot, heat the oil over medium-high heat. When hot, add the cumin and cinnamon sticks and cook, stirring, just until the cumin begins to brown. Add the onions and cook until they begin to brown. Add the turmeric and cook 1 minute. Add the chiles, cilantro, and *masoor dal* and cook several minutes. Add the toma-toes, tomato paste, okra, and water. Stir and bring to a boil. Lower the heat to a gentle simmer and cook 20-25 minutes.

When the *masoor dal* is completely tender, add the lemon juice and season with salt and pepper. Remove the cinnamon sticks. Just before serving stir in the *garam masala*.

Serves 6-8

TINY BLACK LENTILS
WITH FRESH FENNEL AND RED PEPPERS

*These tiny lentils are sometimes labeled French indigo or
French green lentils. Whatever their name, they are characterized by their size,
which is half that of ordinary green or brown lentils, and their dark color. They have a rich
flavor, and because of their small size, they cook in less time than their larger relatives.* ✎ *In this dish,
the warm lentils are marinated, and the fresh fennel and red bell peppers are added when
the lentils have cooled. Technically a salad, I suppose, but this
makes a nice accompaniment to a light entrée.*

1½ cups tiny black lentils, rinsed
3 cups water
⅓ cup olive oil
3 tablespoons lemon juice
3 tablespoons balsamic vinegar
½ teaspoon ground fennel seed
1 teaspoon Dijon mustard
½ teaspoon salt
¼ teaspoon freshly ground
　black pepper
1 cup diced fresh fennel
¾ cup diced red bell peppers
⅓ cup diced mild red or
　white onions
chopped fresh fennel leaves,
　garnish

In a 3-quart saucepan, combine the lentils and water. Bring to a boil and then lower the heat to a gentle simmer. Cook until tender but not mushy, about 20 minutes.

While the lentils are cooking, in a small bowl combine the oil, lemon juice, vinegar, fennel seed, mustard, salt, and pepper.

Drain the lentils and pour them into a serving bowl. While the lentils are hot, pour the oil mixture over them and stir well to coat evenly. When the lentils have cooled, mix in the fennel, peppers, and onions. Garnish with the fennel leaves. Serve at room temperature or serve warm by reheating briefly.

Serves 4-6

*Tiny Black Lentils with
Fresh Fennel and Red Peppers
(recipe this page)*

BAKED CANNELLINI BEANS WITH LEMON AND ROSEMARY

*Garlic, lemon, olive oil, and rosemary indicate the Mediterranean
origin of this marvelous dish. Rosemary is a powerful herb, and too much can impart
a distinct medicinal flavor. I find that fresh rosemary has a gentler taste than dried, and for that reason,
I grow a large pot of it. These plump and savory beans are the perfect accompaniment
to a fish or poultry entrée. (Photo on page 129.)*

1 cup dried cannellini beans
　(2½ cups cooked)
1 medium clove garlic, minced
1 tablespoon olive oil plus extra
　for serving
2 sparse 4-inch sprigs of rose-
　mary, or ½ teaspoon dried
1 lemon
simmering water
salt and freshly ground black
　pepper, to taste

Sort through, rinse, and soak the beans (see Chapter 7).

Preheat the oven to 325°F. Drain the beans and pour them into a 1-quart baking dish. Stir in the garlic, oil, and rosemary. Cut the lemon in quarters and reserve 3 quarters for the garnish. Remove the seeds from the remaining quarter and score its rind with a sharp knife. Squeeze the juice into the beans and stir well; then add the entire quarter.

Add enough of the water to cover the beans and bake, partially covered, 2 hours, or until tender. Check the water level after 1½ hours, and add more water if necessary.

To serve, drizzle a little olive oil over the top, if desired, to add some gloss. Season with salt and pepper. Slice the remaining 3 lemon quarters into wedges and add them as garnish. Serve warm or at room temperature.

Serves 4

BABY LIMA BEAN AND DRIED SHIITAKE MUSHROOM CASSEROLE

*When dried shiitake mushrooms are soaked in hot water, the results are
magically reconstituted mushrooms and a richly flavored broth. That broth forms the base
for the wonderful mushroom gravy in this casserole, and the reconstituted shiitakes add texture and
their own deep, dark mushroom flavor. This dish also uses a roux, a combination of fat and
flour, to thicken the casserole and makes a fine accompaniment to an autumn
entrée of grilled or roasted chicken or stuffed squash.*

2 cups dried baby lima beans
   (4 cups cooked)
2 cups boiling water
1 cup dried shiitake mushrooms
½ cup sherry
2 tablespoons soy sauce
1 tablespoon olive oil
1 tablespoon butter or margarine
1 cup chopped onions
¼ cup flour
¼ cup chopped parsley
½-¾ teaspoon salt
¼ teaspoon freshly ground
   black pepper

Sort through, rinse, and soak the beans (see Chapter 7).

Preheat the oven to 350°F. In a medium-size bowl, pour the water over the mushrooms and soak at least 30 minutes. When the mushrooms are fully reconstituted, remove them from the liquid and reserve the liquid. To prepare the mushrooms, remove and discard the stems and slice the caps thin. Pour the mushroom broth into a 4-cup measuring cup and add the sherry and soy sauce. Add enough water or stock to make 3 cups.

In a large, heavy-bottomed frying pan, heat the oil and butter over medium-high heat. When hot, add the onions and sauté until translucent. Lower the heat and stir in the flour, mixing well to make a roux. Cook, stirring occasionally, 5 minutes to brown the flour.

Pour the 3 cups of liquid into the roux, stirring well. Add the mushrooms and parsley and bring to a boil. Lower the heat and simmer 5 minutes.

In a casserole dish, combine the beans and the mushroom sauce. Stir in the salt and pepper and bake, covered, 1½ hours, or until the beans are tender.

Serves 6

FLAGEOLETS WITH A MIREPOIX

Although flageolets come in several colors, the most commonly
available is a very pale green. These beans are a staple in many French dishes.
They have a delicate flavor that is enhanced by the subtlety of a mirepoix, *a classic aromatic mixture*
used as seasoning in French cooking. A mirepoix is made up of equal parts of finely diced
celery, carrots, and onions and an herb, such as marjoram, thyme, parsley,
or tarragon, cooked very slowly in a bit of butter. (Photo on page 76.)

1 cup dried flageolets
   (2½ cups cooked)
1 tablespoon butter
1 cup diced celery
1 cup diced carrots
1 cup diced onions
1 teaspoon dried tarragon
1 cup stock
salt and freshly ground black
   pepper, to taste

Sort through, rinse, soak, and cook the flageolets by your preferred method until tender (see Chapter 7). Drain.

In a large frying pan with a lid, melt the butter over medium-high heat. Add the celery, carrots, onions, and tarragon and stir to mix. When the vegetables are hot, lower the heat, cover, and cook slowly 10-15 minutes, or until tender, stirring occasionally to prevent browning. Add the flageolets and stock. Bring to a boil, lower the heat, and simmer, covered, 15 minutes. Season with salt and pepper. Serve hot.

Serves 4-5

HOPPIN' JOHN

*I love the ritual aspect of this rice and bean dish. It is
traditionally served in the South at the beginning of the new year. The belief is
that eating Hoppin' John at that time will bring good luck for the rest of the year. And
that belief is strong—I've had southern friends ascribe good or bad years to whether or not they had
Hoppin' John on New Year's Day. But this dish is too good to restrict its consumption to
once a year. It goes well with such traditional southern foods as sweet potatoes and
cooked greens, as well as with ham or chicken. Like many bean dishes,
its taste improves after it's had a chance to absorb flavors.*

1 cup dried black-eyed peas
   (2 cups cooked)
2-3 slices bacon
1 cup chopped onions
1 medium clove garlic, minced
1 bay leaf
pinch of ground red pepper
pinch of ground cloves
½ cup uncooked white rice
1½ cups water or stock
2 tablespoons cider vinegar
salt and freshly ground black
   pepper, to taste

Sort through, rinse, and soak the black-eyed peas (see Chapter 7). Drain.

In a frying pan with a lid, cook the bacon over low heat until crisp. Remove and drain on a folded paper towel. Crumble and set aside.

Add the onions and garlic to the hot bacon fat in the pan. Sauté until the onions are translucent. Add the bacon, bay leaf, red pepper, cloves, and rice and stir to combine. Add the water, vinegar, and black-eyed peas and bring to a boil. Lower the heat, cover, and simmer 30 minutes, or until the rice and beans are tender. Check halfway through and add more liquid if necessary. Season with salt and pepper. Serve hot.

Serves 4

MAIN DISHES

Spicy Black Bean Tostadas
with Eggs and Salsa
(recipe on page 144)

SPICY BLACK BEAN TOSTADAS WITH EGGS AND SALSA

*Brunch should be as much about enjoying your company as
enjoying your food. For this dish, you can prepare everything ahead of time
except a panful of eggs and some lightly crisped tortillas. Just set out the tortillas, beans,
and eggs with bowls of fresh salsa, Monterey Jack cheese, guacamole, and sour cream,
and let everyone build their own tostada.(Photo on page 142.)*

2 cups dried black beans
  (4 cups cooked)
2 cups reserved bean stock
2 tablespoons vegetable oil plus
  extra for frying
1 tablespoon ground cumin
1 tablespoon ground coriander
⅛-¼ teaspoon ground red pepper
1 clove garlic, minced
1 medium onion, finely chopped
1 green bell pepper, finely
  chopped
2 tablespoons tomato paste
¼ cup chopped cilantro
salt, to taste
eight 6-inch corn tortillas
8 eggs, fried, or 1 dozen
  eggs, scrambled
Monterey Jack cheese
Fresh Tomato Salsa, 1 recipe

Sort through, rinse, soak, and
cook the beans by your preferred
method (see Chapter 7). Drain,
reserving 2 cups of the stock.

In a large pot, heat 2 tablespoons
of the oil over medium heat. When
hot, add the cumin, coriander, and
red pepper and sauté 30 seconds.
Add the garlic and sauté, stirring,
30 seconds. Add the onions and
peppers and sauté until the onions
are translucent.

Add the beans, stock, and tomato paste and simmer 20 minutes.
The mixture should have the
consistency of chili. Add water
if necessary. Remove from the heat
and add the cilantro. Season with
salt. Preheat the oven to 200°F.

In a heavy frying pan, heat a
small amount of oil over medium
heat. Add the tortillas and fry
them one at a time on both sides
until they are puffed and crisp.
Drain on paper towels and keep
warm in the oven until serving.

Serve the tostadas topped with
the beans, eggs, Monterey Jack
cheese, and Fresh Tomato Salsa.

Serves 8

FRESH TOMATO SALSA
5 medium tomatoes, chopped
¼ cup chopped cilantro
1 tablespoon red wine vinegar
½ small onion, grated
1 teaspoon bottled hot sauce
salt, to taste
1½ teaspoons sugar, if tomatoes
  are not in season

In a small bowl, combine the
tomatoes, cilantro, vinegar,
onions, hot sauce, salt, and sugar,
if applicable. Let sit at room temperature at least 1 hour.

CURRIED CHICKPEAS

This simple and easy-to-prepare mild curry fills the kitchen with the tantalizing aroma of garam masala, a fragrant blend of several ground, dry-roasted spices. You can find recipes for numerous regional variations of garam masala in any Indian cookbook, but you can also purchase it ready-made. When you buy it, look for the type that comes in a sealed tin and use it within six months, or it will lose its fresh taste. Garam masala is usually added at the end of cooking as a concluding garnish of flavor. ✍ *Since this is a mild curry, I like to serve it with the vibrant and irresistible complexity of Cilantro and Mint Chutney (recipe follows). If you have leftover Curried Chickpeas, purée them in a blender or food processor for a great spread or dip.*

*1 cup dried chickpeas
(2 cups cooked)*
1 cup reserved chickpea stock
2 tablespoons vegetable oil
1 tablespoon black mustard seeds
2 teaspoons turmeric
1 large onion, chopped
1 large clove garlic, minced
1 teaspoon grated fresh ginger
*2 medium potatoes, peeled and
cut into ½-inch cubes*
*1 can (28 ounces) tomatoes with
juice, chopped*
2 teaspoons garam masala
*salt and freshly ground black
pepper, to taste*

Sort through, rinse, soak, and cook the chickpeas by your preferred method (see Chapter 7). Drain, reserving 1 cup of the stock.

In a large pot, heat the oil over medium heat. When hot, add the mustard seeds and turmeric and sauté until the mustard seeds begin to pop. Add the onions, garlic, and ginger and sauté over low heat 5-10 minutes, or until the onions are translucent. Add the potatoes and 1 cup of the tomatoes and cook 10 minutes, stirring occasionally.

Add the chickpeas, stock, and the remaining tomatoes. Cook, stirring occasionally, 30 minutes, or until the potatoes are tender. Add the *garam masala* and season with salt and pepper.

Serves 4

Note: Black mustard seeds are very common in Indian cooking and are available in Asian markets or in the Indian section of a well-stocked grocery store. If they aren't available, yellow mustard seeds can be substituted.

CILANTRO AND MINT CHUTNEY
*1 medium green bell pepper,
roughly chopped*
*⅓ cup lightly packed chopped
cilantro*
*¼ cup lightly packed chopped
fresh mint*
*½ cup grated unsweetened
coconut*
¼ cup low-fat plain yogurt
2 tablespoons lemon juice
½ teaspoon salt
*½ teaspoon toasted cumin seeds,
optional*
½ minced jalapeño chile, optional

In a blender or food processor, combine the peppers, cilantro, mint, coconut, yogurt, lemon juice, and salt, and the cumin seeds and chiles, if using. Process 1 minute, or until pulverized but not liquefied.

MACEDONIAN LIMA BEANS (TAVCHE NA GRACET)

Ask anyone who has ever taught English as a second language, and they'll wax poetic about the class potluck dinners. That's where I got this extraordinary recipe, which comes from Sonia Hot, an immigrant from the former Yugoslavia. Meaning literally "clay pot in the fire," Tavche na Gracet is made of layers of lima beans, prunes, and gently sautéed onions that caramelize to a savory sweetness in the oven. As simple as it is delicious, it's easy to see why this dish has been around for centuries. ✍ *Traditionally, this dish is eaten with a chunk of thick peasant bread. I serve it with a green salad, a glass of red wine, and dreams of the Adriatic.*

2½ cups large dried lima beans
6 cups water
¼ cup plus 3 tablespoons vegetable oil
4 cups sliced onions
3 cups reserved bean stock
1½ cups sliced pitted prunes
3 tablespoons sweet Hungarian paprika
3 tablespoons chopped fresh or dried dill
9 bay leaves
salt and freshly ground black pepper

Put the lima beans in a soup pot, fill the pot with enough water to cover the beans, and simmer 5 minutes. Remove from the heat and drain. Refill the pot with the 6 cups of water and add the beans. Bring to a boil, lower the heat, and simmer 30-40 minutes, or until the beans are tender but not fully cooked.

Preheat the oven to 350°F. While the beans are simmering, in a large frying pan, heat 3 tablespoons of the oil over low heat. When hot, add the onions and sauté until soft and translucent.

When the beans are done, drain them, reserving 3 cups of the stock.

Lightly oil the bottom and sides of a deep-sided 3-quart baking dish. In the dish, layer one-third of the lima beans, onions, prunes, paprika, dill, and bay leaves. Generously salt and pepper the layer and drizzle on one-third of the remaining oil. Repeat this process, making 2 more layers. Pour the reserved bean stock over the top of the casserole to moisten it. There should be enough liquid to almost cover the beans. Add more water if necessary and bake, covered, 50-60 minutes. The beans are done when they are moist and succulent in a thickened, rich sauce. If the sauce is too thin, remove the cover and bake 10-15 minutes more.

Serves 6 as a main dish, 8 as a side dish

top: West Indian Split Yellow Pea Soup (recipe on page 112); bottom: Macedonian Lima Beans (recipe this page)

LENTIL AND RICE POTTAGE

*This is a comfort food of the highest order. Like most
comfort foods, this dish transcends its very ordinary ingredients. It is good
with crisp finger food, such as radishes, carrots, and cucumber sticks, or with
a Middle Eastern coleslaw made of shredded cabbage and a dressing
of lemon juice, olive oil, garlic, and chopped mint.*

2 cups dried green lentils
1 cup uncooked brown rice
1 teaspoon salt plus extra to taste
¼ teaspoon freshly ground black
    pepper plus extra to taste
6⅓ cups water
3 tablespoons olive oil
2 cups minced onions
plain yogurt, garnish
lemon wedges, garnish

In a heavy soup pot, combine the
lentils, rice, 1 teaspoon of the salt,
¼ teaspoon of the pepper, and
6 cups of the water. Bring to a
boil. Reduce the heat, cover, and
simmer 35 minutes, or until the
rice is done.

While the lentils are cooking,
heat the oil over low heat. When
hot, add the onions and sauté
until soft and slightly browned.
Add the remaining ⅓ cup water
and simmer 10 minutes, or until
all the water is absorbed.

Stir the onion mixture into the
lentil mixture. Season with salt
and pepper. Pour into individual
serving bowls. Spoon a dollop of
yogurt over each serving and garnish with the lemon wedges.

Serves 4-6

BAKED BLACK BEAN CUSTARDS WITH TOMATO-CILANTRO SAUCE

*Bake these savory bean-purée custards in individual cups for
an appealing and unusual dish. They have a surprisingly delicate texture,
and their mild seasoning is nicely complemented by the tangy Tomato-Cilantro Sauce.
Cooking mellows the cilantro while still allowing it to stand out. This dish is perfect as
an entrée served with a green salad and some crusty bread or as a side
dish with a light and simple chicken or fish entrée.*

2 cups dried black beans
  (4 cups cooked)
1½ cups reserved bean stock
3 large eggs
3 tablespoons low-fat plain yogurt
1½ teaspoons ground cumin
1½ teaspoons ground coriander
¾ teaspoon salt
½ teaspoon freshly ground
  black pepper
vegetable oil for coating
boiling water
Tomato-Cilantro Sauce, 1 recipe
6 cilantro leaves, garnish

Sort through, rinse, soak, and
cook the beans by your preferred
method (see Chapter 7). Drain,
reserving 1½ cups of the stock.
Preheat the oven to 350°F.

Purée the beans and stock in a
food processor or food mill. In a
separate bowl, beat the eggs,
yogurt, cumin, coriander, salt, and
pepper. Add this mixture to the
bean purée, mixing well.

Coat the insides of six 6-ounce
custard cups with the oil. Divide
the bean purée equally between
the 6 cups, filling them no higher
than ½ inch from the top. Place
the filled cups in a 9-inch by
13-inch baking dish and add
1 inch of boiling water to the pan.
Bake 45-50 minutes, or until an
inserted knife comes out clean.

To serve the custards, remove
the cups from the water bath and
let set 5-10 minutes. Run a thin
knife around the insides of the
custard cups and gently unmold
the bean purée. Serve topped with
warm Tomato-Cilantro Sauce and
a cilantro leaf.

Yields 6 individual custards

TOMATO-CILANTRO SAUCE
1 tablespoon olive oil or
  vegetable oil
1 large clove garlic, minced
3 cups tomato purée
2 tablespoons chopped
  fresh cilantro
salt and freshly ground black
  pepper, to taste

In a saucepan, heat the oil over
medium heat. When hot, add
the garlic and sauté until it turns
golden. Add the tomato purée and
cilantro. Season with salt and pepper. Simmer gently 15-20 minutes.

SPANISH CHICKPEA STEW

*This versatile stew can be served as a main dish over rice or
as an accompaniment to a light entrée. Deep green parsley sprinkled over
this muted red and beige dish makes it visually appealing.*

1 cup dried chickpeas
   (2 cups cooked)
1 cup reserved chickpea stock
1 tablespoon olive oil
3 cloves garlic, minced
1 tablespoon sweet paprika
1 cup puréed tomatoes
salt and freshly ground black
   pepper, to taste
1 tablespoon red wine vinegar
¼-½ cup low-fat sour cream
chopped parsley, garnish

Sort through, rinse, soak, and cook the chickpeas by your preferred method (see Chapter 7). Drain, reserving 1 cup of the stock.

In a large, deep frying pan, heat the oil over medium-low heat. When hot, add the garlic and paprika and sauté 2-3 minutes, or until the garlic begins to turn golden. Add the chickpeas, stock, and puréed tomatoes. Continue to cook over low heat, stirring occa-sionally to prevent sticking, 15-20 minutes, or until the stock has thickened.

Remove from the heat. Season with salt and pepper. Stir in the vinegar and sour cream and top with the parsley. Serve warm or hot.

Serves 4

BRUNSWICK STEW
TWICE REMOVED

*What makes cooking more art than science is the endless tinkering and
invention that goes into it. Sara Robbins, a cook at Moosewood Restaurant in Ithaca, N.Y.,
offers her uncle's special recipe for Brunswick Stew minus the meat in* Sundays at Moosewood Restaurant
*(Simon and Schuster, 1990). This is an adaptation of that delicious recipe, with a bit of meat thrown in—not
the squirrel found in some old recipes for Brunswick Stew, but kielbasa, the delicious Polish sausage
that can now be found in a low-fat version. This stew makes a satisfying dinner served in
shallow soup bowls with a loaf of crusty bread and a fresh green salad.*

1 cup dried black-eyed peas
(2 cups cooked)
2 tablespoons vegetable oil
3-4 medium onions, chopped
(2 cups)
3 cloves garlic, minced
½ cup chopped carrots
½ cup chopped green bell
peppers
1 cup chopped potatoes
2 cups chopped fresh tomatoes,
or 1 can (16 ounces) chopped
tomatoes with juice
2 cups stock
1½ tablespoons molasses or
brown sugar
1½ tablespoons cider vinegar
¼ pound low-fat kielbasa, halved
and sliced ¼ inch thick
2-3 tablespoons chopped cilantro
1½ cups sliced fresh okra, or
1 package (10 ounces) frozen
okra
1½ cups fresh corn, or 1 package
(10 ounces) frozen corn
3 tablespoons Worcestershire
sauce
½ teaspoon bottled hot sauce
3 tablespoons ketchup
salt and freshly ground black
pepper, to taste

Sort through, rinse, soak, and
cook the black-eyed peas by your
preferred method (see Chapter 7).

In a large pot, heat the oil over
medium heat. When hot, add the
onions and garlic and sauté until
golden. Add the carrots and peppers and sauté 3 minutes, stirring
to prevent sticking. Add the potatoes, tomatoes, and stock. Bring
to a boil, then lower the heat to

simmer. Add the black-eyed peas,
molasses, vinegar, kielbasa,
cilantro, okra, corn, Worcestershire sauce, hot sauce, and
ketchup. Simmer over low heat,
stirring occasionally, 30 minutes,
or until the vegetables are tender.
Remove from the heat and season
with salt and pepper.

Serves 6

PASTA WITH BROCCOLI, WHITE BEANS, AND SUN-DRIED TOMATOES

*Pasta's rapid rise in popularity in the last decade is a testament
to its convenience, short preparation time, and remarkable versatility. This
light sauce combines the creaminess of white beans, the sharper taste of broccoli,
and the sweetness of sun-dried tomatoes with an enticing white-wine aroma.*

¾ cup sun-dried tomatoes
1½ cups dry white wine, or
   1 cup dry white wine plus
   ½ cup water
2 tablespoons olive oil
2 teaspoons minced garlic
1¼ cups chopped onions
3½ cups chopped fresh broccoli
½ teaspoon crushed red
   pepper flakes
1½ cups cooked white beans
¼ cup chopped fresh basil
salt and freshly ground black
   pepper, to taste
1 pound bow tie or orrechiette
   pasta
freshly grated Parmesan cheese

With scissors, cut the tomatoes into strips. Put them in a small bowl and pour the wine over them. Soak at least 30 minutes.

In a large frying pan, heat the oil over medium-low heat. When hot, add the garlic and sauté until it turns golden. Add the onions and sauté until they are translucent. Stir in the broccoli and red pepper flakes and sauté, stirring occasionally, 2-3 minutes. Add the tomato mixture, beans, and basil.

Bring to a boil, lower the heat, and simmer 5-10 minutes, or until the broccoli is tender. Season with salt and pepper.

Cook the pasta according to the package directions. Rinse, drain well, and divide into 4 servings. Top the pasta with the vegetable sauce and Parmesan cheese.

Serves 4

Note: When I cut the broccoli for this dish, I cut the florets into pieces about ½ inch long. If the stem has a tough outer layer, I peel it and then slice it thinly so that it will cook in the same amount of time as the florets.

*top: Sicilian Fava Bean Soup
(recipe on page 104);
bottom: Pasta with Broccoli, White Beans,
and Sun-Dried Tomatoes (recipe this page)*

SMOKY CHICKPEA BURGERS

*Smoked cheddar and the sweet nuttiness of pecans give these burgers
an exciting flavor that needs no enhancement. They can be baked for a low-fat finish
or sautéed in a little oil for a delicious toasted brown crust.*

1 cup dried chickpeas
   (2 cups cooked)
2 eggs
¾ cup grated smoked
   cheddar cheese
½ cup pecans, finely chopped
½ cup fresh breadcrumbs
½ cup grated carrots
pinch of ground red pepper
salt and freshly ground black
   pepper, to taste
1 tablespoon soy sauce
2-3 scallions, white and green
   parts, minced
1½ teaspoons ground coriander

Sort through, rinse, soak, and cook the chickpeas by your preferred method (see Chapter 7). Drain.

In a food processor, combine the chickpeas and eggs and process until puréed. Turn out the purée into a bowl and add the cheddar, pecans, breadcrumbs, carrots, red pepper, salt, black pepper, soy sauce, scallions, and coriander. Chill, covered, 2-3 hours. When you're ready to cook the burgers, form this mixture into 6 patties.

If you're baking the burgers, preheat the oven to 350°F and lightly oil a baking sheet. Place the patties on the sheet and bake 20 minutes.

If you're sautéing the burgers, in a large frying pan, heat a little oil over medium-high heat. When hot, place the patties in the frying pan and sauté 3-4 minutes on each side, or until a browned crust has formed.

Yields six 3½-inch burgers

Fava Bean and Onion Stew over Lemony Couscous

*A marvelous combination of spices and long-cooked onions
makes a memorable sauce for fava beans served over a delicate lemony couscous.
If ful medames, a small Egyptian fava, are available, use them. Otherwise,
use the large dried favas more commonly available.*

2 cups ful medames *or large fava
  beans (3½ cups cooked)*
3 tablespoons olive oil
2 large cloves garlic, minced
5 cups sliced onions
1 cup chopped onions
generous pinch of saffron
1½ teaspoons freshly ground
  black pepper
2 teaspoons powdered ginger
1 teaspoon turmeric
¼ teaspoon ground red pepper
¼ teaspoon grated fresh nutmeg
1 teaspoon cinnamon
¼ cup minced cilantro
¼ cup minced parsley
6 cups stock
Lemony Couscous, 1 recipe
plain yogurt, garnish
chopped parsley, garnish

Sort through, rinse, soak, and cook the beans by your preferred method (see Chapter 7).

In a heavy-bottomed soup pot, heat the oil over medium heat. When hot, add the garlic and sauté until it just begins to turn golden. Add the sliced and chopped onions and sauté, stirring often, until they begin to brown. Add the saffron, black pepper, ginger, turmeric, red pepper, nutmeg, and cinnamon. Stir and sauté 1 minute. Add the cilantro and minced parsley, stirring well. Add the beans and stock. Simmer, uncovered, stirring occasionally, 1 hour. Serve hot over Lemony Couscous, topped with yogurt and chopped parsley.

Serves 6

Note: Because some people object to the rather leathery skin of the larger beans, you may want to remove their skin before cooking. This can be done after soaking them overnight or by pouring boiling water on them and allowing them to sit for 1 hour. Use the tip of a paring knife to slit the skin and tear it off, pinching the bean out at the same time.

LEMONY COUSCOUS

2 cups couscous
2¼ cups boiling water
1 tablespoon grated lemon rind
¼ cup lemon juice
salt, to taste

Place the couscous in a large bowl. Add the boiling water and cover. Let steep 10-15 minutes. Add the lemon rind, lemon juice, and salt, stirring to fluff.

Serves 6

SAVORY
KIDNEY BEAN STEW

*Unlike traditional stews that have the meat and vegetables all simmered
together, this stew has three basic divisions: the cooked beans; the meat cooked with wine
and onions; and the sautéed leeks, parsley, and cilantro. The latter group provides a savory flavor packet
that is added at the end for maximum taste. Then the whole dish is finished off with a bit of
lemon juice to give it a lift. It is marvelous with basmati rice and a green salad.*

2 cups dried kidney beans
   (4 cups cooked)
1 pound beef or lamb stew meat,
   cut into 1-inch cubes
2½ tablespoons olive oil
1 medium-large onion, chopped
1 tablespoon flour
½ teaspoon salt plus more
   to taste
1 cup dry red wine
2 cups water
3 leeks, white and green parts,
   chopped (1½ cups)
¾ cup chopped parsley
⅓ cup chopped cilantro
2-3 tablespoons lemon juice
freshly ground black pepper,
   to taste

Sort through, rinse, soak, and cook the beans by your preferred method (see Chapter 7). Drain.

Dry the meat with paper towels so that it will brown thoroughly. In a heavy pan, heat 1 tablespoon of the oil over medium-high heat. When the oil is very hot but not smoking, add the meat and brown it on all sides. Lower the heat and add the onions. Sauté until the onions are slightly browned. Stir in the flour and sauté 1 minute. Add ½ teaspoon of the salt, wine, and water, stirring to dislodge any browned bits in the bottom of the pan. Bring to a boil and then lower the heat to a slow simmer. Simmer, stirring occasionally,

1-2 hours, or until fork tender. Check the liquid level after an hour or so, adding more water if needed.

In a medium-size frying pan, heat the remaining 1½ tablespoons of the oil over medium heat. Add the leeks, parsley, and cilantro. Sauté, stirring frequently 8-10 minutes, or until the leeks are lightly browned and the parsley has darkened.

Add the beans, leek mixture, and lemon juice to the meat. Season with salt and pepper. Serve hot.

Serves 4

BEANS AND GREENS WITH HERBED POLENTA

*Italian comfort food. That's what this combination of creamy polenta,
succulent beans, and sharp greens is. The optional bits of pepperoni add a dash
of spice. You can use any type of cooked bean here. Although many traditional recipes stipulate
that polenta must be stirred without ceasing, I get perfectly acceptable results from
only frequent stirring. Just take care that it doesn't begin to burn.*

Polenta:
1½ cups coarse yellow
    cornmeal
1 teaspoon salt
2 tablespoons mixed fresh herbs
    (rosemary and parsley are
    especially good)
4 cups hot water
olive oil for greasing

Beans and greens:
2½ tablespoons olive oil
1½ teaspoons minced garlic
1½ cups chopped onions
2-3 tablespoons finely chopped
    pepperoni, optional
3 cups chopped Swiss chard, kale,
    or spinach, or a combination
1 can (28 ounces) tomatoes with
    juice, chopped
1½ cups cooked beans
¼ cup chopped fresh basil plus
    extra for garnish
salt and freshly ground black
    pepper, to taste
grated Parmesan cheese

For the polenta, in a 3-quart pot, combine the cornmeal, salt, herbs, and water, making sure there are no lumps. Bring to a boil. Lower the heat and simmer, stirring frequently, 30 minutes, or until the polenta is thick and comes away easily from the sides of the pan.

Grease a large sheet of aluminum foil with the oil and place it on a baking sheet. With a rubber spatula or wet hands, slide the polenta onto the baking sheet, guiding it into a rectangle measuring approximately 8 inches by 12 inches. Make the corners as square as possible. Lay a second sheet of aluminum foil on top and allow the polenta to set at least 30 minutes.

For the beans and greens, in a large, deep frying pan, heat the oil over medium heat. Add the garlic and sauté until it turns golden. Add the onions and pepperoni, if using, and sauté until the onions are translucent. Add the greens and sauté, stirring, until wilted. Stir in the tomatoes and beans and simmer 15 minutes. Stir in the basil and season with salt and pepper.

To serve, cut the polenta into 4 equal rectangles and then cut each rectangle into 4 triangles. Place the triangles on oiled aluminum foil or an oiled grill under the broiler and cook 5-6 minutes per side, or until the exterior is a spotted brown. Remove from the heat. Ladle on the bean mixture and top with the Parmesan cheese and extra basil.

Serves 4-6

BONELESS CHICKEN BREASTS WITH CHICKPEAS, SUN-DRIED TOMATOES, AND MADEIRA

This elegant and unusual dish is an adaptation of a dish by Bahram Bahrami, a chef and caterer of dazzling skill in Austin, TX. Bahram talks passionately about flavor, texture, and technique in cooking the way a composer talks about structure, melody, and harmony in a composition. The cooking technique used in this recipe—cooking ingredients quickly over high heat—is like that of a stir-fry, so it is imperative that all the ingredients are prepared and assembled ahead of time. Do the cooking in a wok or a large nonstick frying pan. ᔆ A rice or grain pilaf and a simple green salad or steamed vegetables with fresh herbs make fine companions to this dish.

¾ cup sun-dried tomatoes
1 cup Madeira
1 tablespoon finely chopped shallots
2 tablespoons olive oil
1½ teaspoons minced garlic
4 skinless, boneless chicken breast halves, julienned
1 red bell pepper, julienned
1 cup cooked chickpeas, drained
3-4 artichoke bottoms, sliced thin, or 4-5 artichoke hearts, quartered
⅛ teaspoon oregano
salt and freshly ground black pepper, to taste

With scissors, cut the tomatoes into strips. In a small bowl, combine the tomatoes, Madeira, and shallots and soak at least 1 hour.

In a wok or nonstick frying pan, heat the oil over high heat. When hot, add the garlic and sauté, stirring, until slightly browned. Add the chicken and sauté 1-2 minutes, or until it has lost its pink color. Add the peppers and chickpeas and sauté 1-2 minutes. When the pan has heated up after this addition, add the tomato mixture, artichokes, and oregano. Bring to a boil and lower the heat. Cover and steam until the liquid is nearly gone, about 10 minutes. Season with salt and pepper.

Serves 4

Boneless Chicken Breasts with Chickpeas, Sun-Dried Tomatoes, and Madeira (recipe this page)

NEW WORLD CASSOULET

*This delicious and deeply satisfying dish may not have
the complexity of a classic cassoulet from the Languedoc region of France,
but on the other hand, it doesn't take three days to make and use six different types of
meat and poultry. ᔪ A simple green salad and perhaps some garlic bread are the only
accompaniments this dish needs. Like most bean dishes, its flavor improves with
age, so it's a good thing to make ahead of time for a dinner party.*

2 cups dried white beans
   (5 cups cooked)
1½-2 tablespoons plus 2 teaspoons olive oil
one 3-pound chicken, cut up
½ pound low-fat kielbasa,
   sliced into ¼-inch rounds
3 medium onions, chopped
2 large celery ribs with leaves,
   sliced
1 large clove garlic, minced
1½ teaspoons dried thyme
¼ cup chopped fresh parsley
2-3 bay leaves
2½ cups dry white wine
2½ cups chicken stock or water
salt and freshly ground black
   pepper, to taste
1 cup fresh breadcrumbs

Sort through, rinse, and soak the beans by your preferred method (see Chapter 7). Drain.

In a Dutch oven or similar large oven-proof stew pot, heat 2 teaspoons of the oil over medium heat. When hot, add the chicken and brown it on both sides. Remove the chicken to a plate. Add the kielbasa to the pot and sauté until slightly browned. Remove the kielbasa. Add the onions, celery, garlic, and thyme to the pot and sauté until the onions begin to brown. Then add the parsley, bay leaves, wine, and stock, stirring to dislodge any browned bits in the bottom of the pot. Add the beans, chicken, and kielbasa and simmer, covered, 1½ hours.

The cassoulet is done when the chicken falls off the bones. You can either leave the chicken as it is in pieces or remove the skin and the bones, leaving chunks of very tender chicken. Season with salt and pepper.

For the traditional baked-crumb topping, preheat the oven to 375°F. Combine the breadcrumbs with the remaining 1½-2 tablespoons of oil and spread the topping over the top of the cassoulet. Bake 30-40 minutes, or until the crumbs have formed a toasted crust.

Serves 6

PIGEON PEAS WITH SOFRITO AND SAFFRON RICE

*Sofrito is a flavoring used in areas of the Caribbean under
Spanish influence. You can make it at home (recipe follows) or buy it canned
or frozen in the Caribbean food section of the supermarket or in ethnic markets. It is a very
useful ingredient to have on hand for adding flavor to soups, stews, and casseroles.
You can find the aji dulce peppers in Latino markets. (Photo on page 132.)*

1 cup dried pigeon peas
   (2½ cups cooked)
1 tablespoon vegetable oil
3 cloves garlic, minced
2 cups chopped onions
2-3 heaping tablespoons Sofrito
1 tablespoon tomato paste
1 can (14½ ounces) tomatoes,
   drained
salt and freshly ground black
   pepper, to taste
Saffron Rice, 1 recipe

Sort through, rinse, soak, and
cook the peas by your preferred
method (see Chapter 7). Drain.

In a large frying pan, heat the
oil over medium-low heat. When
hot, add the garlic and sauté until
it just begins to turn golden. Add
the onions and sauté until the
onions are slightly browned. Add
the *Sofrito* and sauté 1-2 minutes.
Mix in the tomato paste and cook
2 minutes. Add the tomatoes and
crush them with the back of a
spoon. Add the peas. Simmer 15
minutes. Season with salt and pepper and serve with Saffron Rice.

Serves 4-6

SOFRITO

These directions are for a very
basic *sofrito*. There are as many
variations as there are cooks, some
sautéing the vegetables with salt
pork, ham, or tomatoes. If you
make a large amount of *sofrito*,
freeze it in ice cube trays. Each
cube is about 2 tablespoons'
worth, a useful amount in recipes.

1 green bell pepper, chopped
1 medium onion, chopped
1 clove garlic, minced
¼ cup chopped cilantro
1 cup roughly chopped small
   sweet peppers, such as Italian
   frying peppers or aji dulce
1 tablespoon vegetable oil

Purée the bell peppers, onions,
garlic, cilantro, sweet peppers, and
oil in a blender or food processor.
As a rule of thumb, to use the
sofrito, sauté 2 tablespoons of it for
a minute or two in a small amount
of olive or vegetable oil. Add a
tablespoon of tomato paste and
cook for 2 minutes.

Yields about 1½ cups

SAFFRON RICE

In the Moosewood Restaurant
kitchen, Bob Love, one of the
cooks, showed me this method of
cooking rice without measuring
the water. I don't understand why
this method works, but it works
consistently for me. Basmati rice is
especially good with this dish.

generous pinch of saffron
pinch of sugar
1½ cups white or basmati rice
water
salt, to taste

In a mortar, pulverize the saffron
and sugar.

In a saucepan, mix the saffron
and sugar with the rice. Pour in
enough water to cover the rice to
the depth of the first knuckle on
your index finger. Bring to a boil,
lower the heat to simmer, and partially cover. Simmer 25-30 minutes, or until the water has been
absorbed. Turn off the heat, cover
the pan completely, and let the
rice steam 5 minutes. Season with
salt, fluff, and serve.

Yields 4 cups

PASTA FAZOOL

*As a young cook leafing through Italian cookbooks, it was some time before
I realized that the recipes I had read as Pasta e Fagioli were one and the same as my old
neighborhood favorite, "Pasta Fazool." I suppose there are as many pasta fazools as there are cooks.
My favorite version is this recipe, adapted from a restaurant in Buffalo, N.Y., that is locally famous
for this dish. I was first introduced to this Italian soul food by visiting friends who arrived with take-out
containers of it. ✍ This pasta fazool has no tomatoes in it. Long cooking creates a dish
of succulent beans in a rich and creamy vegetable gravy served on ditalini, which are
very short tubes of pasta. It is topped with grated Parmesan cheese and always
served with pickled hot peppers on the side.*

1 cup dried chickpeas
1 cup dried large lima beans
2 tablespoons olive oil
2 cups chopped onions
2 tablespoons minced garlic
1 jar (7½ ounces) roasted
   peppers
½-1 teaspoon crushed red
   pepper flakes
7 cups water
salt, to taste
2½ cups dried ditalini pasta or
   very small tubular pasta
freshly grated Parmesan cheese

Soak the chickpeas and lima beans by your preferred method (see Chapter 7). Drain.

In a soup pot, heat the oil over medium heat. When hot, add the onions and garlic and sauté until browned. Chop the roasted peppers. Add the chickpeas, beans, chopped peppers, red pepper flakes, and water to the onions. Cook 1½ hours, stirring occasionally during the last 30 minutes. Add more water if necessary to thin to a gravylike consistency. Season with salt. Taste and adjust the seasonings if necessary.

Cook the pasta according to the package directions. When tender, drain and spoon into shallow soup dishes. Ladle the fazool mixture over the pasta and top with Parmesan cheese.

Serves 6

WHITE CHILI

*Three different types of peppers plus a generous amount
of black pepper give this chili an irresistible and tantalizing spiciness. It has an
unusually fresh, rather than a simmered-for-hours, taste. I like to serve it in shallow bowls topped
with sour cream and chopped cilantro, with hot cornbread and a garden salad on the side.
When you cook this dish, prepare and assemble the ingredients in advance so
that they will be ready to go into the pan at the right moment.*

2 cups dried Great Northern
   beans (4 cups cooked)
¼ cup olive oil
2 cups finely chopped scallions,
   white and green parts
3 boneless, skinless chicken
   breast halves, cut into ¾-inch
   cubes
3 tablespoons flour
4 cups chicken stock
3 cloves garlic, minced
3 celery ribs, minced
3 Anaheim, Hungarian wax, or
   other mildly hot chiles, seeded
   and sliced thin
1-3 jalapeño chiles (depending on
   your taste for heat), seeded
   and sliced thin
2 red bell peppers, julienned
1 tablespoon ground cumin
2 teaspoons freshly ground
   black pepper
1 tablespoon fresh thyme, or
   1 teaspoon dried
2 tablespoons minced cilantro
sour cream, garnish
minced cilantro, garnish

Sort through, rinse, soak, and cook the beans by your preferred method (see Chapter 7). Drain.

In a heavy-bottomed soup pot or a Dutch oven, heat 2 tablespoons of the oil over medium-high heat. When hot, add the scallions and cook, stirring, until wilted. Add the chicken and cook, stirring occasionally, until it appears white on the outside. Sprinkle with the flour and cook, stirring, allowing the flour to brown slightly. Add the stock, scraping the bottom of the pan to dislodge any browned bits. Bring to a boil, lower the heat, and simmer 20-30 minutes.

While the chicken is simmering, in a nonstick frying pan, heat the remaining 2 tablespoons of oil over medium heat. Add the garlic and sauté briefly just until it begins to turn golden. Add the celery and sauté 1 minute. Add the chiles and bell peppers and sauté until they begin to wilt. Add the cumin, black pepper, thyme, and cilantro and sauté 1 minute.

Add the beans and the pepper mixture to the chicken. Bring to a boil, lower the heat, and simmer 5 minutes. Garnish each serving with a dollop of sour cream and the cilantro. Serve hot.

Serves 6-8

METRIC CONVERSIONS

Dry Weights

U.S. Measurements	Metric Equivalents
¼ ounce	7 grams
⅓ ounce	10 grams
½ ounce	14 grams
1 ounce	28 grams
1½ ounces	42 grams
1¾ ounces	50 grams
2 ounces	57 grams
3 ounces	85 grams
3½ ounces	100 grams
4 ounces (¼ pound)	114 grams
6 ounces	170 grams
8 ounces (½ pound)	227 grams
9 ounces	250 grams
16 ounces (1 pound)	464 grams

Liquid Weights

U.S. Measurements	Metric Equivalents
¼ teaspoon	1.23 ml
½ teaspoon	2.5 ml
¾ teaspoon	3.7 ml
1 teaspoon	5 ml
1 dessertspoon	10 ml
1 tablespoon (3 teaspoons)	15 ml
2 tablespoons (1 ounce)	30 ml
¼ cup	60 ml
⅓ cup	80 ml
½ cup	120 ml
⅔ cup	160 ml
¾ cup	180 ml
1 cup (8 ounces)	240 ml
2 cups (1 pint)	480 ml
3 cups	720 ml
4 cups (1 quart)	1 liter
4 quarts (1 gallon)	3¾ liters

Length

U.S. Measurements	Metric Equivalents
⅛ inch	3 mm
¼ inch	6 mm
⅜ inch	1 cm
½ inch	1.2 cm
1 inch	2.5 cm
¾ inch	2 cm
1¼ inches	3.1 cm
1½ inches	3.7 cm
2 inches	5 cm
3 inches	7.5 cm
4 inches	10 cm
5 inches	12.5 cm

Temperatures

Fahrenheit	Celsius (Centigrade)
32°F (water freezes)	0°C
200°F	95°C
212°F (water boils)	100°C
250°F	120°C
275°F	135°C
300°F (slow oven)	150°C
325°F	160°C
350°F (moderate oven)	175°C
375°F	190°C
400°F (hot oven)	205°C
425°F	220°C
450°F (very hot oven)	230°C
475°F	245°C
500°F (extremely hot oven)	260°C

SOURCES

The following list contains the catalogs that I am most familiar with as sources for a variety of dried legume seeds and the dried legumes themselves. Many of them provide a free or low-cost education in successful vegetable growing.

SEEDS

Abundant Life Seed Foundation
P.O. Box 772
Port Townsend, WA 98368
(360) 385-5660

Dedicated to preserving biodiversity and supporting sustainable agriculture with specific emphasis on providing seeds of open-pollinated and heirloom varieties not otherwise available commercially. Large list of bean cultivars.

Bountiful Gardens
18001 Shafer Ranch Rd.
Willits, CA 95490-9626
(707) 459-6410

A good source of information on biointensive gardening methods. Lists several runner beans.

Fedco Seeds
P.O. Box 520
Waterville, ME 04903-0520
(207) 873-7333

Specializes in untreated seed for northern gardens and offers five sizes of attractively priced packets in their densely packed informational catalog.

Fox Hollow Herb and Heirloom Seed Co.
P.O. Box 148
McGrann, PA 16236
(412) 548-7333

This family-run company always has an interesting list of beans available.

Garden City Seeds
778 U.S. Highway 93 North
Hamilton, MT 59840-9448
(406) 961-4837

Specializes in successful short-season varieties; offers an educational catalog with good growing information.

Johnny's Selected Seeds
Foss Hill Rd.
Albion, ME 04910-9731
(207) 437-4301

A reliable source of seeds and growing information for northern gardeners since 1974; offers a select group of standard and heirloom dry and shell bean varieties.

Native Seeds/SEARCH
2509 N. Campbell Ave. #325
Tucson, AZ 85719
(520) 327-9123

Specializes in conserving traditional crops of the Southwest. Fascinating catalog offers growing information, recipes, and seeds adapted to desert conditions. Offers lima, tepary, fava, runner, common, and wild bean seeds. No phone orders.

Park Seed Co.
1 Parkton Ave.
Greenwood, SC 29647-0001
(800) 845-3369

Offers a large variety of seeds adapted to growing in the South. Nice dry bean selection.

Pinetree Garden Seeds
Box 300
New Gloucester, ME 04260
(207) 926-3400

Over 750 varieties of reasonably priced seeds.

R. H. Shumway's
P.O. Box 1
Graniteville, SC 29829
(803) 663-9771

A great compendium of old-fashioned and modern varieties slanted toward those that grow well under southern conditions, including lima bean and Southern pea varieties.

Salt Spring Seeds
P.O. Box 444, Ganges P.O.
Salt Spring Island, B.C.
Canada V8K 2W1
(259) 537-5269

Lists the largest commercial selection of bean and grain varieties in North America. It has an amazing array of favas and soup peas, as well as beans.

Seed Savers Exchange
3076 North Winn Rd.
Decorah, IA 52101
(319) 382-5872

This worthy organization is a network of members interested in the preservation of traditional open-pollinated (nonhybrid) seeds. Membership brings three fascinating and informative publications a year, one of them a 430-page book that lists 11,000 seeds and tells how to obtain them from their growers. Membership is $25. There is also a special $20 membership fee (no questions asked) for those with reduced incomes.

Seeds Blum
HC 33 Box 2057
Boise, ID 83706
(800) 528-3658

This catalog is in a class by itself, maintaining a personal style that, with its fine writing and whimsical illustrations, enlightens, educates, and amuses.

Seeds of Change
P.O. Box 15700
Santa Fe, NM 87506
(800) 957-3337

A large and interesting selection of organically grown, open-pollinated seeds are offered in a beautifully produced and educational catalog. Large bean selection, including fava and tepary beans.

**Southern Exposure
Seed Exchange**
P.O. Box 170
Earlysville, VA 22936
(804) 973-4703

Although the name of this seed company suggests their attention to seeds for hot and humid areas, there is much here to interest gardeners in other sections of the country.

Territorial Seed Co.
P.O. Box 157
Cottage Grove, OR 97424-0061
(541) 942-9547

Offers a very informative catalog with a slant toward varieties that do well in the Northwest. Has 'Painted Lady' runner bean and a dwarf variety.

Vermont Bean Seed Co.
Garden Lane
Fair Haven, VT 05743-0250
(802) 273-3400

This company has specialized in beans since its founding and offers a large assortment.

MAIL-ORDER BEANS

Gallina Canyon Ranch
P.O. Box 706
Abiquiu, NM 87510
(505) 685-4888

Elizabeth Berry offers a variety of dried beans grown on her ranch, as well as seeds, dried chiles, and recipes.

Phipps Ranch
P.O. Box 349
Pescadero, CA 94060
(800) 279-0889

The Phipps family offers an astonishing range of over 90 dried beans, lentils, and peas. They also offer cereals and grains, herbed vinegars, and herb and spice blends.

Wood Prairie Farm
49 Kinny Road
Bridgewater, ME 04735
(800) 829-9765

The Gerritsens offer a choice of five organically grown dried bean varieties attractively packaged in burlap bags.

BIBLIOGRAPHY

Ashworth, Suzanne. *Seed to Seed: Seed Saving Techniques for the Vegetable Gardener*. Decorah, Iowa: Seed Saver Publications, 1991.

Baron, Robert C. and Henry S. Commager, eds. *The Garden and Farm Books of Thomas Jefferson*. Golden, CO: Fulcrum Publishing, 1987.

Brown, Wesley and Amy Ling, eds. *Imagining America: Stories from the Promised Land*. New York: Persea Books, Inc., 1991.

Bubel, Nancy. *The Country Journal Book of Vegetable Gardening*. Brattleboro, VT: Country Journal Publishing Co., 1983.

Campbell, Joseph. *Historical Atlas of World Mythology*. Vol. II, parts 2 & 3. New York: Harper and Row, 1989.

Coleman, Eliot. *The New Organic Grower's Four-Season Harvest*. Post Mills, VT: Chelsea Green Publishing Co., 1992.

Cost, Bruce. *Bruce Cost's Asian Ingredients: Buying and Cooking the Staple Foods of China, Japan and Southeast Asia*. New York: William Morrow & Co. Inc., 1988.

Creasy, Rosalind. *Cooking from the Garden*. San Francisco: Sierra Club Books, 1988.

Evans, Ianto. *A Gardeners Guide to Fava Beans*. Cottage Grove, OR: The Fava Project, 1992.

The Fairy Tales of the Brothers Grimm. Trans. by Mrs. Edgar Lucas. New York: Doubleday, Page and Company, 1909.

Foster, Nelson and Linda S. Cordell, eds. *Chilies to Chocolate: Food the Americas Gave the World*. Tucson: University of Arizona Press, 1992.

Garden Seed Inventory, Fourth Edition. Comp. by Kent Whealy. Decorah, Iowa: Seed Saver Publications, 1995.

Graves, Robert. *The White Goddess*. New York: Farrar, Strauss and Giroux, Inc., 1986.

Hurt, R. Douglas. *Indian Agriculture in America: Prehistory to the Present*. Lawrence: University Press of Kansas, 1987.

Kaplan, Lawrence. "New World Beans." *Horticulture* (October 1980): 43-49.

Lewandowski, Stephen. "Doihe'ko, the Three Sisters in Seneca Life: Implications for a Native Agriculture in the Finger Lakes Region of New York State." *Agriculture and Human Values* (Spring/Summer 1987): 76-93.

McCully, Robert S. *The Enigma of Symbols in Fairy Tales: Zimmer's Dialogue Renewed*. Lewiston, NY: The Edwin Mellen Press, 1991.

McGee, Harold J. *On Food and Cooking*. New York: Charles Scribner's Sons, 1984.

Morrow, Barbara. "The Rebirth of Legumes." *Food Technology* (September 1991).

Nabhan, Gary. *Enduring Seeds: Native American Agriculture & Wild Plant Conservation*. Berkeley, CA: North Point Press, 1989.

———. *Gathering the Desert*. Tucson: University of Arizona Press, 1993.

———, ed., *Desert Plants*. Vol. 5, Number 1 (1983).

National Gardening Association Staff. *Gardening: The Complete Guide to Growing America's Favorite Fruits and Vegetables*. Reading, MA: Addison-Wesley, 1986.

Phillips, Roger and Martyn Rix. *The Random House Book of Vegetables*. New York: Random House, 1993.

Reed, Charles A., ed. *The Origins of Agriculture*. The Hague, Netherlands: Mouton, 1977.

Reynolds, Peter. *Farming in the Iron Age*. London: Cambridge University Press, 1976.

Root, Waverley. *Food*. New York: Simon and Schuster, 1980.

Sass, Lorna J. *Great Vegetarian Cooking Under Pressure*. New York: William Morrow and Co., Inc., 1994.

Simpson, B. B. and M. Connor-Ogorzaly. *Economic Botany: Plants in Our World*. New York: McGraw-Hill, 1980.

Smartt, J. and N. W. Simmonds, eds. *Evolution of Crop Plants*. Essex, England: Longman Scientific and Technical, 1995.

Smith, Bruce D. *The Emergence of Agriculture*. New York: W. H. Freeman and Co., 1995.

Tannahill, Reay. *Food in History*. New York: Crown Publishers, 1989.

Traveller Bird. *The Path to Snowbird Mountain*. New York: Farrar, Straus and Giroux, Inc., 1972.

Wilson, Gilbert, ed. *Buffalo Bird Woman's Garden: Agriculture of the Hidatsa Indians*. St. Paul, MN: Minnesota Historical Society Press, 1987.

Withee, John. *Growing and Cooking Beans*. Dublin, NH: Yankee Publishing, 1980.

INDEX

INDEX

Associate Publisher: Helen Albert

Editorial Assistant: Cherilyn DeVries

Editor: Jennifer Renjilian

Designer: Henry Roth

Layout Artist: Suzie Yannes

Photographer except where noted: Boyd Hagen

Illustrator: Rosalie Vaccaro

Indexer: Diane Sinitsky

Typeface: Goudy

Paper: 70-lb. Somerset Gloss

Printer: Quebecor Printing/Hawkins, New Canton, Tennessee